Cut the Crap Trader

Steven Aubin

CONTENTS

Acknowledgements

This book was made possible with the help of two very good friends: Hadaf Zubi and Kristof. They painstakingly edited Cut the Crap Trader, and professionally elevated the book. Thank you both, I owe you! I also have to thank my life partner Jirat Manapeancharoen, who supported me every step of the way. She created the cover and some thought-provoking cartoons found throughout the book. As you open this book, remember that nothing great is accomplished alone.

PREAMBLE

Greed and fear are the two words that define the beginning of most stock trader's journey. What brings us here together? - Is it a path to riches, an alternative lifestyle free from the shackles of the 9 to 5 rat race, or is it our fascination that motivates us? My long and bumpy road could have been so much easier with some clear concise help. With so many books, articles, gurus, pundits and financial news out there, it's exceedingly difficult to find a concrete path to successful trading. Countering arguments confuse and discourage you, pushing you away from the goal of becoming a trader. Information overload is overwhelming, we want to start with bite sizes. I want to share my own experiences working from a beginner retail trader, all the way up the food chain to becoming a licensed professional trader. In essence, having been through many pitfalls and rubbish information out there, I want to "Cut the Crap" from your learning process, and get you well on your way to trading.

Every professional trader or investor has a process or methodology they follow. This booklet takes a top-down approach, leading you all the way from coming up with ideas to executing a successful trade. I wanted to write this booklet because most trading books lack a system that strategically plans a trade **entry and exit while reducing risk**. A strong trading plan boosts confidence and encourages a beginner trader to pull the trigger and get the trade on. Having said that, all that matters to the profitability of your trade is what happens **after** you take on the position. The same trade can be profitable and ruinous, depending on your timing. The central theme of this booklet is: <u>Cut your losses quickly to fight another day</u>.

ROADMAP FOR CUT THE CRAP TRADER

What is out there to trade?

Fundamental and Technical Analysis

Charting and Formations

Generating Ideas and Watchlist

Trading plan

Executing the Trade

Monitoring

Portfolio Construction

Business Cycle and Economic Factors

The Intangibles of Trading

CHAPTER 1: A TRADER'S WORLD

To be a successful trader, you'll always be striving to reach a perfect state of mind. For a trader that means being disciplined and somewhat robotic. There are two phases to any trade, the idea and the position. The first step is the idea - picking something that eventually makes you millions. When I say "something," I mean selecting one of the plethora of financial instruments that will either rise or fall accordingly. This game is filled with different approaches: thematic traders, industry specific traders, volatility traders, etc. The key is to find an angle that works for you. Taking different methodologies and fusing them together into a systematic approach. The first phase is all about IDEAS, and generating them. Predicting the future, involves thinking about what will grow, what will fall apart, and what instruments to use to profit from events. Eclectic and esoteric people seem to dream up the best ideas. There aren't many pure artists on Wall Street, which is a shame. Apart from random ideas, you will need a systemic engine to produce ideas day after day that will bear fruit.

Phase two is all about protecting capital and maximizing gains. In other words, money management. Like all successful traders, the one rule I follow is "live to see another day". Your idea will work or it won't, plain and simple. I'm paraphrasing this one but "nothing ever good started bad".

What that means is that if you begin a trade that starts out a loser, you either need to get out ASAP or limit your position size (i.e. if you can handle the losses and have a high degree of conviction around your idea). If you take nothing more than this message into your trading, we'll both be laughing together in the end.

One bullshit term that is all over the Internet is "Managing risk". What that really means is "How do I protect myself and profit the most once a trade is on?" During phase two, there is no room for imagination. Planning, either on paper or in your mind, must be plotted out beforehand, and executions followed systematically. You need to ask yourself "At what price points will I dump my holdings?" and remain committed to that number. Survival is not only about sticking around and retaining capital, it's an opportunity to test ideas, and implement different strategies until you reach your 'Eureka' moments.

Greed and fear will constantly be whispering on either one of your shoulders. They are both your greatest enemies. Avoid your emotions and stick to the plan, and do not deviate unless it's Plan B. All the thinking takes place before the purchase. Once the trade is on, your emotions will rush-in to distract you. In order to win at this game, you'll need a plan, and you'll need to follow it. Otherwise, the trade will control your every waking moment, filling your day with lunacy, joy and madness. Random trading leads to financial ruin, and is an expensive lesson. When something isn't working, relieve your stress by dropping or reducing the position, regroup and start again. By accepting defeat, you can move on.

This booklet begins by exploring different investment vehicles, from the common stock to more exotic routes. Before getting started, it's good to know what's out there. Fundamental and technical analysis provide clarity on price levels, movement and company valuations. Without the basics you won't even know what you're looking at or looking for. Once you've grasped how the two forms of analysis work, you need to pull the trigger and buy - that process is examined step by step in the pages that follow. The goal here is gaining enough knowledge and confidence to initiate and then exit trades at the best possible points.

CHAPTER 2: WHAT'S ON THE MENU?

In the beginning, your problem will be nailing-down something to buy. But first you need to know what's out there, and match your risk tolerance to the right investment. For example, someone just starting out shouldn't play the options gauntlet. Why not? Well, on top of a higher risk profile, options simply have more moving parts that confuse newer traders. That isn't to say you won't play options once you're comfortable, but it means that for beginner traders a simpler and cleaner approach will yield more success.

When buying and selling financial instruments, people generally have two different objectives: **capital growth or income**. The younger you are the more risk you can take on because you have more runway to get back on your feet. Unconventional thinking makes people rich when the appropriate amount of risk is taken. Emotions creep-in when more pressure and risk are applied. You should feel steady, at ease, and in control with any investment vehicle you choose. The vehicles listed below range in complexity. Most beginner traders would do well to stick to ETFs at first. After several months, you'll feel more comfortable venturing into different investments.

Exchange Traded Funds

Exchange-traded Funds (ETFs) have become a strong alternative to mutual funds for various reasons. Briefly, the Management Expense Ratio (MER - the fee paid by the purchaser) is comparably lower, but ETFs are traded on actual exchanges so brokerage commissions can add up. Discount brokers have now evolved to a point where many ETFs can be traded commission-free, meaning you only pay the MER to the ETF company. Mutual funds are typically more expensive, require minimum holding periods, minimum unit purchases, and distribute income differently with less tax advantages. Avoid mutual funds like the plague! ETFs are usually liquid and no minimum purchase is required. ETFs provide many options and ways to play the market. ETFs started off by tracking broad market indices such as the S&P 500 and TSX, but have since evolved into sector-themed instruments and even leveraged ETF products that use loans for added exposure. Theme ETFs can for example track the price of oil or bundle different oil companies. Managers generally aggregate different companies, bonds or futures/options contracts to produce a fund. The attractive features include diversification, avoiding individual companies and playing a theme instead of a company. Horizons, an ETF management company, created a Marijuana ETF in early 2017, which provided an opportunity for marijuana enthusiasts to participate in a growing industry without the risk of buying a small company that could go bust. ETF managers shuffle stock positions, and drop non-performing companies, which is a bonus for an investor because it eliminates the need to manually re-adjust their portfolio.

The biggest ETF advantage is **protecting yourself from anomalies, horrible earnings and other events that crush a company's profitability**, which in turn sinks the stock price. Wilan (Now Quarterhill), a company that acquires patents and then sells the rights, caused me many mornings of misery waking up to 30-40% price drops. Their company relied on winning lawsuits against patent infringing companies, which rarely went their way, especially when taking on giants like APPLE. This was a rookie mistake, but taught me never to buy rollercoaster companies, because it's not worth it. With diversification comes less risk, but less reward as well. ETFs are malleable instruments that allow you to participate where you otherwise couldn't, such as the futures market, precious metals, currencies and bond markets.

Foreign Exchange (Forex) and Commodities

Unlike company shares, trading currencies and commodities is less predictable due to price volatility. The price gyrates around a longer-term mean, making your job as a trader more difficult. However, extreme prices eventually turn around in major corrections, perfect for a patient treasure hunter. Stocks can sometimes ascend for decades, as where a currency cannot. Currency exposure is the most important factor for commerce and overseas trading. Prices can only take so much pressure, capitalist forces such as exchange costs come into play reversing price movement. You can play currencies directly on a Forex (Foreign Exchange) trading platform or through ETFs on the major exchanges. In Canada, we have DLR.TO, which tracks the American dollar vs the Canadian dollar. If you are trading in currency ETFs, MER's still apply unlike direct Forex trading platforms. I'd recommend picking up 'Forex for Dummies', a straight forward book with helpful hints. Personally I've avoided the perilous journey into Forex as leverage (borrowed money), is the name of the game. Modest movements can wipe you and your grandchildren out. In January 2015, the Swiss National Bank abandoned its ceiling against the Euro, and the Swiss Franc skyrocketed blowing up millions of individual accounts and banks including FXCM and Citi incurring hundreds of millions in losses. Currencies usually move slower than other asset classes, causing the entire industry to use excessive leverage. Tiny moves compound into gigantic dollar moves. Using ETFs can help you avoid destructive situations, if you can find the right currency pair to trade at the right time.

Access to Commodity trading can be trickier due to them being physical assets and under a different regulatory regime (The CFTC vs. the SEC). If you want direct access, you'll need a platform that deals in futures contracts where you can trade at specific price points, which is a zero-sum game. There is always a seller/buyer for each contract and a winner/loser at a set date. Capital reserve requirements are higher for mark-to-market responsibilities at the end of every day, so the futures market is definitely not for beginners. Another option is purchasing an ETF that tracks the price of a commodity such as gold, oil or natural gas. You aren't forced into a set date when a contract comes due, because you can sit on it and hold. However, ETFs can degrade if they are using-leverage to exaggerate price performance, such as some ETFs that track 2X or 3X the movement of an underlying commodity. Fund companies running these commodity ETFs want you to buy, and in return you incur a cost (MER), generally higher for leveraged ETFs. Nonetheless, as the **ETF degrades you can SHORT SELL taking advantage of a drifting lower price**. For further ETF research look into Horizons, Ishares, BMO, Vanguard, and PowerShares. Targeting companies that produce the commodity itself is another strategy, i.e. buying Goldcorp for Gold, Wheaton Corp for silver, or Encana for natural gas, which can also pay generous dividends. Alternatively, managers aggregate similar companies together such as junior gold miners and large oil ETFs. Companies have frailties with moving HUMAN parts. If you're targeting a commodity like platinum, a purer play with fewer variables is beneficial. Always perform a **chart analysis before purchasing any ETF, because you want to be aware of degradation and contango.**

Figure 2.1: Exposure to Commodities

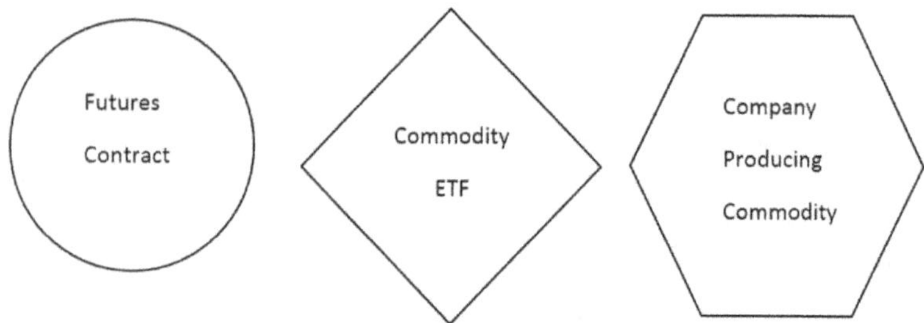

Geography of Markets

Emerging market and **country ETFs** open the door to distant and often inaccessible markets. Purchasing a stock directly from an overseas exchange can cost hundreds just for commissions. However, if you do decide to buy overseas, choosing an international bank like Citibank or HSBC charge far lower commissions due to their worldwide presence. In 2016, the Russian economy and stock market collapsed. As an individual retail investor, how could you have benefitted from this overreaction? You might know some great companies but how would you start picking away at them, your access is highly restricted. That's when you turn to a Russian ETF trading in New York (e.g. RUSL or RSX), playing Russia as a theme. Almost every country is available for you to trade, as fund companies put together a variety of blue chip stocks (Large cap) from a particular country providing breath and diversity. A country's performance rotates from highs to lows just like sectors in the economy. Seeking Alpha's provides a country ETF page, which sorts out monthly and yearly performance. Like the "Dogs of the Dow Theory", which argues buying the poorest performing stocks on the Dow will eventually turn and outperform in the coming year, country ETFs may work similarly. One year Ireland (EIRL) will fly, and Brazil will cry. The next year Brazil (EWZ) could be the world star performer.

Bonds and Fixed Income

For the longest time I avoided bonds, because I didn't think they made much sense pumping out a pathetic 3% coupon taxed as interest. Bonds like currencies and commodities have a ceiling on price. Bonds have two countering parts: the coupon and the bond face value, which change inverse to each other. As a bond price rises the coupon (yield) reduces, meaning for every dollar purchase of a bond the income ratio received falls. Bond face values always start at 100 ('Par'), but when they are above par say 103 they trade at a premium and distribute less income. If a bond trades below par say at 90, it trades at a discount with a higher distribution in relation to price. The coupon doesn't change, but the prevailing bond price changes the yield you receive. Much like when a stock price drops, the numerical amount of the dividend stays the same but the yield is higher now in relation to the lower stock price. Apart from the mechanics, bonds are another asset class to profit from at SPECIFIC points in time. Bonds go through phases of buying and selling depending on interest rates. When interest rates rise, bonds fall and when rates fall bonds rise, areas of great profit. For historical reference, global bond yields are at the lowest rates in human history (2017), which makes a bond price rally very **unlikely** at this point in time.

You can buy and sell bonds on the market just like stocks. However, transactions are more cumbersome as accrued interest is an upfront cost owed to the seller, which you recapture when the coupon is distributed (don't forget commissions). Generally, junk bonds or low grade bonds yield higher returns than investment-grade issues, but can be difficult to get rid of. When a company is falling apart their bond prices also begin to fall, and can lose triple AAA ratings by Moody's or other ratings agencies. Pension funds and other large institutions are not able to hold non-investment grade bonds, and therefore dump distressed debt (junk bonds). Nevertheless, buying distressed debt or bottom-feeding can be a win-win situation for traders. On the one hand, if the company bounces back you'll receive a high yield and bond appreciation. **On the other hand, the company goes bust and as a debt holder you get paid first before everyone else at 100 even though you bought at a discount well below face value**. Worse case is that you lose everything, which is extremely rare because bonds are secured debt. In January 2016, Teck Resources was a clear example where their bonds and stocks were trading at record lows, bouncing back as a rocket performer. To purchase distressed debt be sure to phone your broker, and go over the transaction.

Bond ETFs help investors move quickly into bond themed plays such as a turn-around in bond prices. Barclays has the TBT ultra-leveraged short bond ETF and non-leveraged TBF short 20-year treasury. These ETFs are referred to as **INVERSE** products that act in the opposite direction of a market. For something less exotic, BMOs aggregated bond ETF that yields about 3% is somewhere to park money or play long-term bonds without having to buy bonds directly. Instruments are available for both sides of a bond trade.

Equities (Stocks)

The equity class of assets and stocks bear the most variety. You could waste a good sum of time searching for the right company. Companies are generally separated by size and maturity. **Blue chip** stocks are well-established companies with steady growth and income, and are widely held. For this reason, regulators allow investors to borrow more capital when using Blue chip stocks as collateral in exchange. Heavy traders that rely on leverage (loans), usually hold blue chip stocks allowing them to put more money to work elsewhere. Cisco or Suncor in Canada are blue chip companies, as are most companies in the DOW JONES Industrial Average. These companies are considered to be more resilient when compared against small cap stocks in correction periods (bear markets). Wealthy investors, pension funds and sovereign wealth funds park their money in the crown jewels of the market. Nevertheless, blue chip companies don't last forever. Alcoa, an aluminum company, was around for decades before being relegated from the DOW, plummeting to new lows and going through several reorganizations ('Reorgs'). Solid, long-standing companies are only so good till they aren't.

Small capitalized companies or even micro stocks have the greatest upside, but any major small cap trader has several defunct or bankrupt stories. Investing in small caps is said to be gambling, which most of the time is essentially blind target practice. That aside, small caps are where the money is, with gains in the ranges of 1000%. Big fish versus small fish, the veterans of the game come to gobble up what little money the beginners have. The high flying names are found on the most active small cap lists, where fortunes are lost and made. My cautious nature has kept me and my money away from them, especially penny stocks. Marijuana penny stocks had atmospheric gains with the advent of legalization. Canadians of every denomination drove into them making a buck or two thinking they were genius, only to give back their gains. The phenomenon of pump and dump manipulation is synonymous with penny and small cap stocks. A market maker/manipulator is king and rules this pond, being able to move the stock price. This is an impossible task among blue chips stocks, with multi-billion dollar market caps.

Pure equity players usually keep their capital in cash or stocks, seeking value and upside movement. Money is in constant flux, gyrating from one place to another, from over-valued to undervalued. Being conscious of **where money flows is paramount,** and you want to avoid sectors that are hollowing out. In 2017, the healthcare sector experienced a massive downturn where money quickly escaped into other sectors such as mining companies like Teck Resources. **Anticipate where capital will move to next, which can be a different country, sector or company**. Below (Figure 2.2) are the major sectors where money flows to and from:

Figure 2.2

Financial - Healthcare - Technology - Metals and Mining - Industrials - Telecom - Utilities

Income and dividend investing has evolved dramatically since the systematic depression in interest rates manufactured by central banks. I have friends who were pushed into all sorts of exotic investments to yield more income. Baby boomers without fortified pensions NEED to find income elsewhere. This brings us to Dividend bearing companies, preferred shares, REITs (Real Estate Investment Trusts) and income ETFs. Company dividends and yield percentages can be found by using simple screeners on news websites like Yahoo finance or TMX Money. Capital appreciation isn't the priority with dividend-payers, but rather it is the income that can be sustained and raised over a period of time. **Debt and payout ratios** are far more important here; how much of the company's profits are going toward dividend payment? Comparison is important, so if two companies are paying a yield of 8% but company ABC has a payout ratio of 120% and company XYZ is 40% of net earnings, which is the better purchase? Obviously company XYZ is far more sustainable and can even increase their dividend. Paying anything over 90% of net earnings is dangerous for dividend longevity. Debt due is another consideration that takes precedence over dividend payments. Debt illustrates other burdens the company may have, even possible bankruptcy. REITs, banks, and utility companies have steady cash flow derived from society's NEEDS, which generate healthy dividends.

Dividends are distributed monthly, quarterly, and sometimes annually. DRIP (Dividend Reinvestment Program) re-invests dividends into company shares **commission-free**, executed through treasury shares or on the open market. You must purchase the shares before the ex-dividend date to be awarded the dividend – yes, this means the date before the ex-dividend date to get the benefit of the monthly, quarterly or annual dividend. However, note that shares typically fall after a distribution. The thought process being the company has lost value dispensing cash reserves leading to an immediate fall in the value of its shares. Excessive payouts and yield are a red flag when accompanied with a falling stock price. Stay away! Don't get caught like I did, because you can lose 10 years' worth of dividends in a day! Don't be greedy chasing yield, because when something is too good to be true, it is. In fact, investors are sometimes denigrated as 'yield pigs' – greedy guzzlers at the dividend trough who get slaughtered far too often because they don't look for sustainable yields.

Options and Derivatives

Once you've elevated from a novice trader, you can move into the world of derivatives or more commonly named Options. An Option is what the name suggests – it is an option to make a purchase or not. Options are contracts between two parties. One party sells the option/contract and the other party buys it. So the contract is purchased for a **premium**, which gives the holder the right to buy or sell an underlying asset from or to the seller of the option. As the buyer of an option, a Call option gives you the right to buy something at a certain price from the seller. A Put gives you the right to sell at a certain price. Generally speaking, options writer/sellers collect income (or the 'premium'), whereas the purchaser of the option pays a premium to have the right to a future action. Thousands of YouTube videos would have you think people exercise the right to buy or sell, however the overwhelming majority of options holders sell the contract to another trader/investor or allow the option to expire worthless.

Options **track** an underlying asset, usually a stock or index. When the underlying asset rises, the option premium will rise, and vice versa. However, options premiums rise quickly in volatile market environments, meaning a possible market sell-off. **Traders want to protect their positions and vigorously buy options**. For example, if you own Apple for the long haul, you might not want to sell it when the price is dropping. So you purchase a Put to protect your position. If Apple craters, you can force another party (exercising your put) to purchase your Apple stock at a higher predetermined price or just sell the contract to another trader. This kind of strategy is considered **hedging** (protecting a position), profiting from either way the market moves. Sometimes positions stagnate. For years, Bank of America (BAC) didn't move an inch. Nevertheless, using a simple **covered call option** would produce some additional income while you hold a BAC-type company that is moving sideways. You cover yourself by owning BAC stock and selling a call option at a price above the market, while collecting income, and possible stock appreciation if the buyer exercises their option. Options are all about using simple math to create a win-win situation.

Time is very valuable when trading options, as every contract has an expiration date leaving the contract worthless. When purchasing options, the rule of thumb is to buy as close to the money as possible (strike price matching the present underlying stock), and with as plenty of time left on the contract as possible (months to years). When selling/writing options, sell the contract far out of the money and for the least amount of time, by weeks to months. In both circumstances, you give yourself more or less time to win. Lastly, options contracts deteriorate at light speed, and losing increments of 10% - 30% a day is normal. However, the upfront money required to buy a contract is less in comparison to buying the underlying asset such as Google trading near $1000. Once the price starts climbing, the contract will move dollar for dollar with the asset, leading to enormous gains. In summary, the world of options trading can be exciting and profitable, but only weigh your "options" out once you've become a seasoned trader.

Short Selling Equities

Short-Selling is the **borrowing** of an equity (stock) from your dealer, and selling into the market. You do this when you are betting that a stock will deteriorate and want to profit from a falling price or hedge (protect) a position you already hold from loss. A bizarre transaction for most beginners to wrap their heads around! Brokers allow you to borrow certain stocks and return them in the future. Try not thinking about the money involved, just the physical shares and you'll have a better understanding. The maximum profit from any short position is the cost at the time of borrowing. Say you borrowed $10,000 worth of shares. That would be the absolute total you collect if the stock went to ZERO (remember, you are short-selling so you gain when the stock depreciates). Your **losses** from a short sell aren't capped however, which could potentially be **exponential** along with the dividend payments you make when shorting. Imagine the pain if you shorted Facebook or Google!

Keeping things simple, short selling is the opposite of buying, because a trader profits from a falling stock price instead. In a systematic bear market, shorting keeps you alive and making money, be sure to set up a margin account with your broker. The contrary is true in a bull market, where short-sellers suffer from a "short squeeze." As more buyers step in, the market goes higher and higher putting pressure on shorts. Eventually, the short-sellers give up and cut their losses by purchasing and returning the borrowed shares, which snowballs pushing prices even higher.

When I first started trading, it took me awhile to get my head around the conceptual short sell. A better question to always ask yourself: "Is this a good time to be shorting?" Stocks drift, slowly moving upward step by step. A losing short position is to be EXITED quickly to avoid damaging portfolio pain. Brokers won't risk their money for you, and positions will be called (a broker will literally cover your position without asking as you are using their money to short-sell), leaving you no choice and a throbbing loss. Nevertheless, as stocks rise step by step, they can violently fall like a broken elevator. Take advantage by short selling and profiting at an accelerated rate. Timing is everything, so wait for the market to show you a loss before piling into a short position. There's nothing dumber than guessing when a stock will meltdown, so wait instead for the long red bars (candlesticks are discussed later). A precursor can be when a float has a high Short %, meaning investors are short-selling the company. This usually indicates bearish sentiment, in other words the sharks are circling. All major regulators produce a monthly report outlining the amount of short-selling for each individual stock.

Trading Volatility

The VIX Index is a measure of **volatility** (fear gauge) similar to a cardiac monitor at the hospital. When options trading jumps, so does the VIX (located in Chicago at the CBOE). The VIX gyrates between 10 and 15 during low volatility environments, but during a systematic failure can move to 80 (Figure 2.3). The VIX index cannot be directly bought, so the closest way to trade it are options contracts that track the index's movement. There are two types of Index options: European, meaning they can only be exercised on the expiration date at a pre-determined point in time. American options may be exercised at any time before expiration. Nonetheless, with both types, you can still sell the appreciated contract to another trader at any time. For most people, the more practical way to get exposure is through long VIX ETFs (VXX). Inverse VIX ETFs rise if volatility is low.

Volatility ETFs are known to use leverage, which expedites value degradation. Be very cautious when acquiring these products. Short selling is my rebellious choice when it comes to volatility, far more opportunity.

Figure 2.3

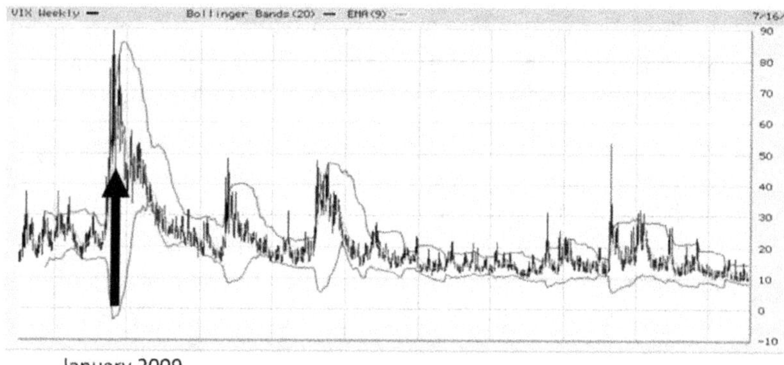

January 2009

CHAPTER 3: RATIOS AND THE BASICS

Starting from the top-down, traders look at stock market **indexes** for overall market health and performance. Examples of indexes include the NASDAQ, the TSX or the NIKKEI in Japan. Various companies are put together to form any given index depending on the structure of the market itself. In Canada, financial and energy companies dominate the market. Consequently, the TSX index composition is highly skewed. Most indexes are based on market capitalization (size in dollars), meaning how much the company is worth on the market, and can be considered a **composite** of the overall market. **Averages** such as the DOW are different, since they are based on the stock prices, not actual value. The DOW Jones Average tracks the 30 biggest or stable companies known as "Blue chip" stocks on the NYSE and is based on equity price, which can be misleading. Large numbered stocks on the DOW can easily sway the Index. Indexes are also known as **benchmarks** for professionals and investors to compare their returns. We're aiming to be way ahead of the average, so it is imperative to keep track of your relevant domestic index. No company can avoid systematic risk in a given index, not even ETFs which are an aggregate of many companies. Indexes set the overall climate of the market. It's vital to ask yourself should I be shorting (selling) or going long (buying) according to the market (Index)?

Ratios (Multiples) are our Thermometer

Price/Earnings (P/E) ratio indicates a lot about a company's current level of activity, growth, future prospects, sector, and maturity. Facebook and Amazon have high P/E ratios in the 100s, which is a result of high stock prices and much smaller earnings per stock. Meanwhile, McDonalds and Ford are around a P/E of 10 or lower. This is Growth vs Stable established business. **Value** investors are people looking for a steal and profess to "buy low, sell high." **Growth** investors aren't as interested in P/E valuations, because they want to join the ride and speculate on future higher earnings. P/E ratios primarily indicate if a company is cheap or expensive relative to other companies. In a Bull market, stocks are rising and forever hitting new highs. As the process escalates, stock P/Es go higher and higher, and at one point value investors no longer see "value" in owning something so expensive. P/E ratios are the fundamental building block of the markets.

Price/Book (P/B) ratio compares the price of the stock to its bare bone worth (Tangible assets). Every company has a book value once you break apart all the pieces into property, trademarks, technology, etc, and sell them off, which gives you a dollar value. A company's stock maybe trading at a value below or above the book value. When a P/B ratio trades below book value you have a number under 1 such as 0.50, which indicates the company is trading at half its net worth. When the ratio is a P/B of 2 the companies is trading at two times the company's net value. Value investors and traders use this to identify stocks which are trading well below their actual worth, which is a great opportunity known as "the margin of safety".

Ratios are meant to attract attention, and are the beginning of the process. They help you understand what's up with a company. David Dremen wrote a book called "Contrarian Investment Strategies," which thoroughly outlines ratios and the power behind them. He essentially proves low P/E and P/B stocks perform best over the long term. This result has also been found by the famed investor Joel Greenblatt. While a masterpiece and cornerstone in my approach, both investors admit that for extended periods of time, buying low ratio stocks may not work. Greenblatt, for example, suggests that his value approach works over three-year holding periods, but not necessarily for any given year within that period. Value investors and Dremen's contrarians are continually scouring for undervalued stocks, a longer play approach. Do not underestimate the gains made from overlooked and undervalued companies.

CHAPTER 4: THE IMPORTANT NUMBERS

We aren't aspiring accountants, but many gurus have said "know your numbers." One of Warren Buffet's indicators is Return on Equity (ROE), which is Net income divided by shareholder's equity. Depending on the industry, ROE can be from single low digits to 50%. Buffet makes a point of using ROE due to the inability of a company to **distort** the numbers. As investors we put some faith into management, but always as little as possible. We can't "pray" for high returns, because we "need" a high degree of certainty. **ROE provides a clear number on how well a company is performing**, since it reveals the net income produced by the shareholder equity. In other words, the net profit produced by the amount of money invested. A consistent 20% ROE is a healthy starting point.

"Debt" - the evil word for commoners, and the lifeblood of the rich. Before getting into bed with a company, you want to know what they owe. A company with ZERO debt cannot go bankrupt, and can live on for a long time. Technology, utility, and mining/energy companies have heavy debt burdens due to the upfront capital required for development. General discretion is used here, because some mature companies have little to no debt, while others have serious debt. Ask yourself, do they have a proven concept, and can they service the debt?

Sector and industry debt comparisons assist an investor in differentiating whether a company is ordinary or exceptional. Debt ratios also help when pondering the choice between two companies. In any case, the next step is to compare debt (liabilities) to assets so that we can determine **whether the company is at least worth what they owe**. Distressed debt (discounted bonds) illustrate a company with financial troubles. For example, bonds start at a face value of 100, but can fall below face value to 80, 70, or even 50. This signals a possible opportunity, or a screaming "stay away." Bonds trading at a deep discount can pay lucrative yields, just as Russian and Brazilian bonds did in 2016. In that case, both bond classes rebounded, and investors made a fortune.

The bottom line is that low debt reflects a company's resilience, which is their ability to bounce back and survive throughout challenging times. The oil market of 2016 saw hundreds of companies fail, so who survived? Well, that story is still being written, but highly indebted companies are long gone.

A company's **Cash** position provides a buffer for any unforeseen circumstances, but can also be used to pay dividends or take advantage of opportunities such as 'share buyback'. Some experts say allocate the available cash to more investments, and put the money to work. Smart CEOs won't just throw money at inefficient expansion and unsustainable growth. For example, pharmaceutical companies Valiant and Concordia, among others, burned through cash, and took on more and more debt. All for increasing revenues that were shallow and inevitably doomed. A higher Cash position versus debt indicates an ability to survive and also take advantage of acquisitions, and new technologies.

Increased **Earnings Per Share** (EPS) over a period of time establishes the company's track record. Analysts are asking themselves: have EPS been growing every year, and what are the expected EPS in the coming years? EPS alone do not provide much useful information, but are imperative for valuation ratios such as P/E. Hitting an EPS below or above analysts' expectations often determines which way the stock goes. So the combination of **earnings and expectations** is what's important. Earnings reports are required quarterly throughout the year, and heavy trading takes place during these seasons. Traders position themselves all around price points, some call it speculation or gambling. However, tracking insider trading can foreshadow the resulting earnings. Analysts throughout the industry will pump out reports forecasting what earnings are to come. A consensus is built with various voices, and when expectations are missed stocks can crumble significantly. I generally stay away from trading during earnings season, but will quickly **initiate a trade once a report is published**. A stock generally continues in a prevailing direction after a positive or negative event of consequence. Momentum accelerates similar to when a train begins to speed-up, since the mass of the train thrusts it further. Implied volatility also increases during earnings season, profitable for options traders.

Accountants and directors control the fundamental analysis in the trading/investing arena. My top-down approach requires me to start with fundamentals, and macro ideas. World events, trends, and the business cycle all enter the equation. However, I'm skeptical at times with analysts' opinions and hearsay. Fundamental Analysis gives us solid numbers and statistics to work with. However, as discussed, the numbers are only useful with proper comparisons, sector/industry perspective, and a deep understanding of valuations within each designated business.

CHAPTER 5: INDICATORS, WIZARDS, AND SELF-FULFILLING PROPHECIES

Unlike fundamentals, technicals are all about price points. People claim to have the winning "systems" or approach that work best, and that will make millions. However, excessive technical analysis looks more like voodoo or having faith in the writings of a 16th century philosopher. Technical analysts tend to turn valid information into noise. Keeping a technical strategy simple is the right approach. Something that can be applied again and again producing profits. Don't get caught up in the perfect system, but use tools that make real world sense to you. Whenever considering a technical indicator, think to yourself, where would this apply in the real world?

Support/Resistance Levels

Figure 5.1

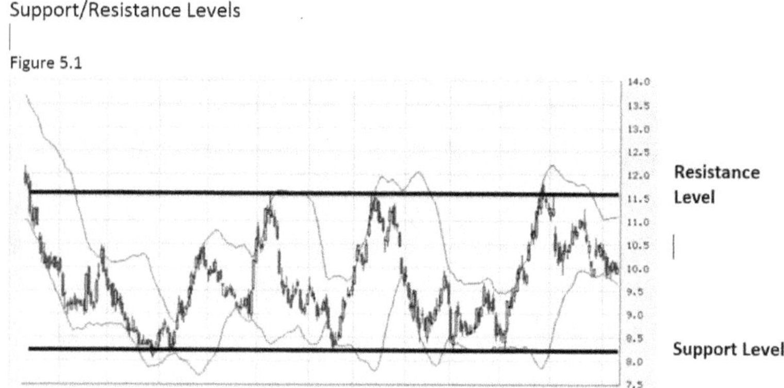

"Price is king," but what does that mean? Through charts, you can see people's thoughts and emotions, so it's a picture of what's going on. To start, let's discuss **resistance** levels (top of band selling) and **support** levels (bottom of band buying). These levels are the building blocks of technical analysis. Support/resistance levels can persist over years, and even decades. Higher volume trading occurs around major levels, but various levels are present throughout long-term charts. When resistance levels are broken to the upside, a **breakout** can occur, where a new **trend** is established. Downward breaking of support levels usually shows bearish pressure. Long red bars on a chart confirm a selling environment, which is perfect for short selling. These events usually occur during earnings season or after news reports. However, news agencies such as CNBC and Bloomberg try to label every major stock move based on an event, but oftentimes no cause is evident. When a stock is rocketing upward, that tells you someone is buying for a reason. In technical analysis, the reason behind price movement isn't what's important, but the movement itself is. Especially when volume is working in congruence with price, don't fight it. **Price shows you what's really going on**, and when you observe that, ask yourself, "should I be buying or selling?"

Before moving on to more detailed explanations of pivot points and stock-picking, we need to go over my top barebone essential technical indicators. The stars don't have to align perfectly. The key is to establish a plan and pull the trigger when appropriate, and when probabilities are stacked in your favor.

Upper Indicators (integrated into the chart)

Moving averages show us where a stock price is trading relative to set data points over a period of time. Common moving average periods are 20, 50 and 200 days. Figure 5.2 shows a 50 day moving average. Personally, I feel a 50 and 200 day moving average gets the job done. Traders are observing if the price is above or below the moving average, and trying to profit from the implications. When prices break through moving averages, trading momentum can pick up, in the same way as around support/resistance levels. A psychological barrier is broken related to price and sentiment consensus. Simple averages work well as a chart overlay, helping us to confirm other indicators. On their own, moving averages are a passive lagging indicator at best, and therefore should be a compliment and not the central thesis to an investment strategy.

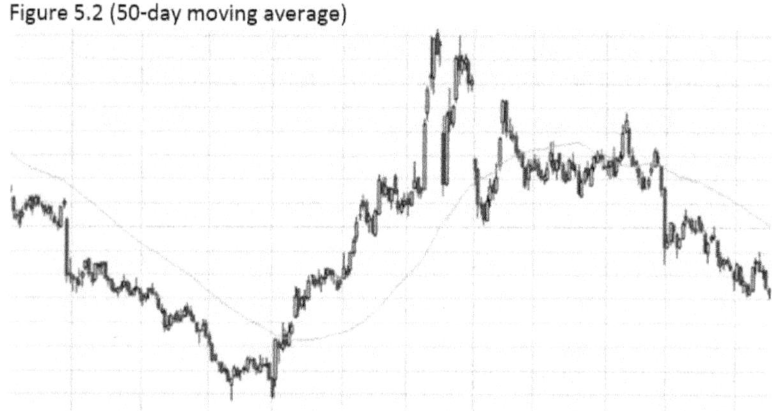

Bollinger bands were created by John Bollinger, a technical trader. The bands use two moving averages - one above and one below the price level. However, one standard deviation is then added and subtracted to both averages, producing a channeling effect. The result is a volatility indicator that lets traders know about market conditions. Price data concerning the equity is usually found within the two bands. When the price is following the top band, it's in a bullish formation and vice versa on the lower band. Even more important is the pinching of the bands, which indicates a pivot point or break out, especially when the price has been sideways for several months. When the price surmounts either band to an extreme, this indicates a direction reversal.

Figure 5.3 (Bollinger Bands)

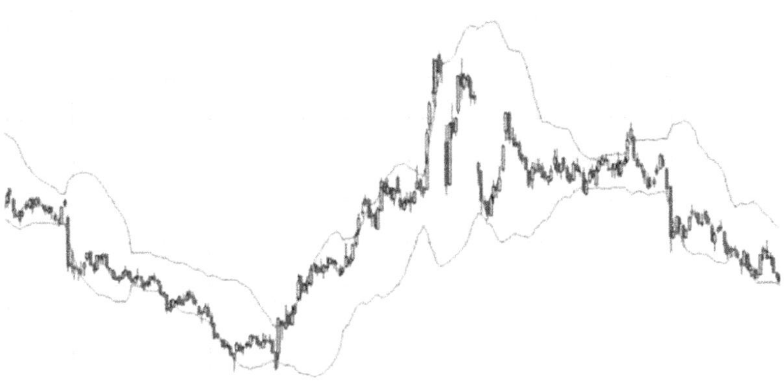

Candlesticks

Japanese Candlestick patterns were invented by Japanese Rice Trader Munehisa Homma in the 18th century, who is clearly a genius we all have to thank. Unlike other tools, candlesticks illustrate intraday movement on a long term chart. People's emotional rollercoasters are carved into candlesticks. Before moving on further, let me explain what an individual candlestick tells us. The price extremes of the day are shown as a "wick" on the top and bottom. A solid bar/rectangle appears in the middle shown as either red or green for the day, an indication of price gaining or dropping. The top and bottom of the bar/rectangle tell us the opening or closing price. Figure 5.4 does a better job at explaining candlestick intricacies.

Figure 5.4

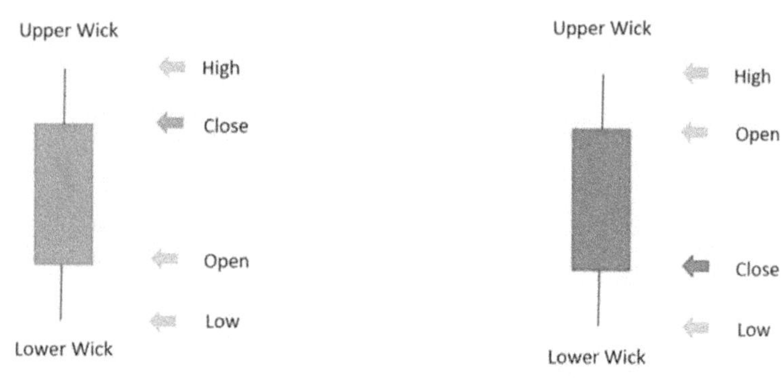

Figure 5.5 (3-month candlestick pattern)

Wicks work congruently with support/resistance level. They show where traders have pushed the market, or where they were testing and fishing the waters. Wicks confirm levels by highlighting **failures** to move higher or lower. This happens with resistance level selling and support level buying. In both cases, the wicks indicate a climax in price. Figure 5.6 shows the price action for Canopy Growth in Canada, a cannabis grower. The climax pattern with the shooting star wick clearly shows exhaustion, and is confirmed three months later with a bounce off resistance levels (double top).

Figure 5.6 Climax Pattern (exhaustion)

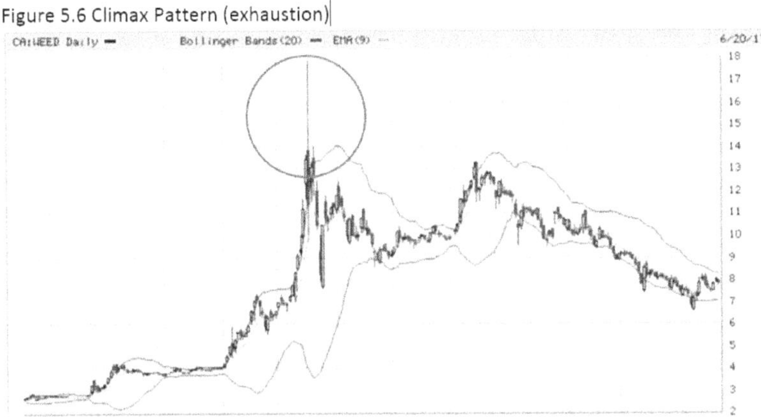

Specific Candlesticks to Watch for:

A **Doji** shows uncertainty in price - an equal amount of sellers and buyers push wicks in opposite and counter-balance directions. The opening and closing prices remain the same creating a cross, a strong indicator of a potential reversal. Discretion and context should be applied here, as Dojis do not act alone but provide a forecast. A long green bar the day after shows strong bullish character. You need to observe the formation around the candlestick and work them in with other indicators. Candlesticks raise the probabilities of either a continuation or reversal.

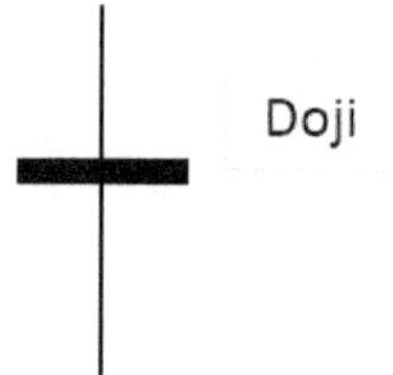

Hammer formations indicate a reversal from bearish to bullish, especially after a long bear market. A bottoming out will occur, whereby investors panic and/or computers initiate trades selling extreme amounts of stock. The reversal starts when buyers step in changing the story upward. Heavy volume accompanies these moves. Within chaos there is opportunity, and **when people are running away that's the time to take another look.**

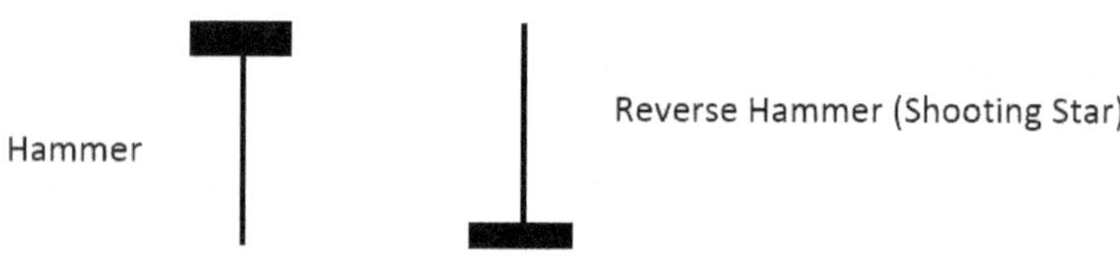

A **Shooting Star** (Reverse Hammer), works similarly to a hammer candlestick but indicates a bearish signal. It's a topping out formation, and best confirmed with heavy volume after a long bull market. Stocks almost always move faster down than up, so for short-sellers shooting stars are indispensable. Figure 5.6 captures a great example of a morphed shooting star, where Canopy hit an extreme of $18.00 and collapsed quickly thereafter. People rush into these trades not wanting to miss out, only to get caught in a vacuum with very few bids where the price collapses to 'clearing prices.'

Long RED bars represent days of continual and confident selling, from higher opening prices, down to much lower closing prices. Earnings reports, forward earnings, analyst downgrades and deleterious news can all cause a stock to fall quickly. Nevertheless, a large investor may also be affecting a stock's price by unloading a position for several reasons. For example, when a modelled target price is achieved or when forecasted earnings growth is met. Neither explanation matters - LONG RED BARS are always a sell signal in my books. Once a stock falls well below your purchase price, you'll be mentally stuck. Get out early before you've lost too much blood. **The number one rule in this book is to retain your capital by selling losing positions quickly.** We accomplish this with a trading plan, which is thoroughly discussed later. Figure 5.7 shows a long red bar after a stock has climaxed, the sell-off is painful for anyone still holding.

Figure 5.7 Climax Pattern 2

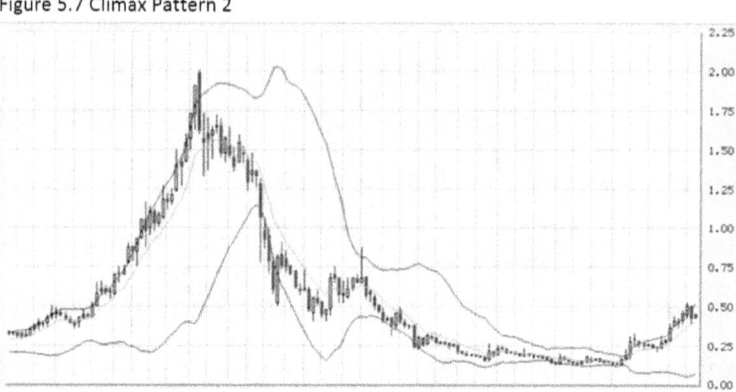

Lower Indicators (below the chart)

Upper indicators provide the most important information concerning price. However, lower indicators are necessary to **confirm** your hypothesis. Deeper pricing analysis provides traders with the confidence and knowledge to get a trade on and more importantly, when to get out. Lower indicators deserve a prolonged discussion which is beyond this booklet's scope. Specific tradable indicators are touched on here, but I encourage every reader to dig deeper into each indicator. **Take what you can use and move on**.

Volume is the amount of stock being bought or sold within a set amount of time. The market open (9:30am) and close (4:00pm) have the heaviest trading volumes. Industry players and the professionals dominate these times, essentially placing bets. The pure day traders will take on positions in the morning and dump them by the close. You need to be well aware of these periods, and **understand where the volume**

is pushing the price. Volume confirms many upper indicators, signaling market conviction. Don't fight the crowd, don't fight the market, just move with it. Long candlesticks in either direction with heavy volume demonstrate trend validation. Industry players have access to a deeper market which retail traders can only dream of. Therefore, we need to follow their lead, heavy volume. Linda Bradford Raschke, a trading genius, says to always stick with high volume names because that's where the action and price moments are, which is bread and butter for traders.

Momentum shows the power (force and speed) behind price movement. Momentum precedes price, which is immensely useful as the majority of lower indicators lag price movement. Momentum works similarly to this analogy: a ball that has been hit hard and fast will move quickly at the beginning continuing on a path forward until losing speed and stopping. The initial event creates a certain amount of energy that dictates the result. In the markets, when momentum is in play and the stock is being accumulated on heavier-than-average volume. Positive aftershocks usually follow by pushing the stock price upward because all of the weak sellers have been bought-out and it takes a higher and higher price to convince the remaining stock holders to sell their shares. Do not confuse technical momentum with momentum trading strategies. A company with an extremely strong trend in an upward direction would be considered a momentum trading strategy, essentially jumping into a trade that is rising very fast.

Relative Strength Index (RSI) is based on price action over a predetermined time period. The target time can be measured over any number of days e.g. 10, 14, or even 50. The price data is then put together to show relative strength from one point in time to another. RSI is incredibly useful for exhibiting **divergence from a trend**. For example, when the stock price is going up but the RSI is falling, it indicates a possible precursor signal for an impending price collapse. The RSI is a relative level measurement. This means that the average line plot is at 50, but moves to a positive position of 80 and negative position of 20. However, when these **extreme values are hit** (20 or 80), a reversal can be close. 'Mean reversion' plays a big role in price gyrations. This is a statistical concept that simply contends that prices move back to an overall average within a given period of time. Nothing goes up or down forever, and even minor corrections are necessary in a bull market. The crossing above or below an RSI of 50 indicates a changing trend, but must endure and follow through sustainably. The dwindling strength of a bull or bear market can usually be detected by a weakening RSI value. Many quantitative traders use mean reversion to build their predictive models.

MACD and **DMI** are indicators I use on occasion to confirm market theories. Briefly, DMI compares buyers and sellers, with an overlay line showing the strength of a trend. MACD utilizes a combination of exponential moving averages (cross over indicators) and histograms to discover bearish/bullish signals. They are complex tools that are useful if implemented correctly and should be researched further by curious traders.

Figure 5.8 Lower Indicators

CHAPTER 6: CHARTING OUR LINES AND IMAGINATION

When tracking a stock's performance, how far back should we go? Once you have identified an asset to purchase, go back as far as you can 5, 10, 20, 30 years. If the company was around during the time of the dinosaurs, what was the price? When working with data, first isolate the long term support and resistance levels, then the mid-term and short-term. Ascertain how many buyers are below or above these levels, and forecast what people will do if the price reaches these levels. Do buyers tend to dry-up at a certain price, causing the price to drop? This is a resistance level. If buyers keep entering the market at this level and price breaks-through on the upside, then this is a bullish signal. Traders and investors need to identify bullish character [higher highs and higher lows] OR bearish character [lower lows and lower highs]. A step-like structure can provide long-term home run trends.

Critics of technical analysis say the approach is self-fulfilling, however no logical person can deny the **psychological** pressures exhibited by traders, which are measured through charting. Understanding behavioral **pivot points need to be observed and respected for opportunity**. Support and resistance levels highlight areas of importance. Figure 6.1 is an ETF tracking the TSX index. You can clearly see resistance at $23.50 and support at $17.00. Stocks are traded by humans, and humans want to trade near round numbers. This is not an isolated example. Every market and stock out there has points of support and resistance.

Figure 6.1

Time-Honored Charting Patterns:

Channeling formations are stock prices moving up or down through a geometric channel indicating a strong trend, where momentum is moving in a set direction (Figure 6.2). Traders will jump into these trends until they reach a reversal and move in the opposite direction, ending the bullish trade.

Figure 6.2 (Channeling)

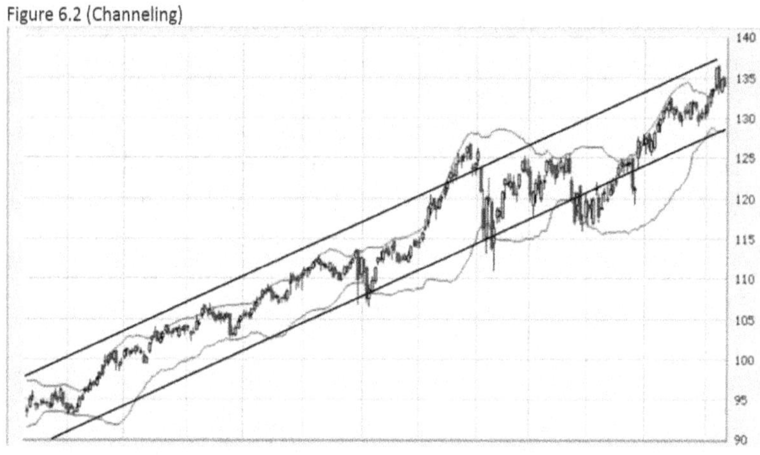

Double topping (Figure 6.3) patterns are bearish, signaling a vacuum in confidence. People are no longer willing to pay a higher price, becoming fully valued - confidence in a new high is lost. The opposite is true for a **Double bottom**, where eager investors jump into a trade, having seen the price move down to valuable levels. If a stock on your watch list confirms a lower level and doesn't sink below it, it's time to begin buying. It'd be like watching your favorite shoes go on sale, not buying them and then kicking yourself for it. However, when the price drops again, your instinct says to buy, causing the price to rise and forms the second bottom. Double formations confirm the true market perception of the stock's minimum value and are extremely useful entry points.

Figure 6.3 (Double top)

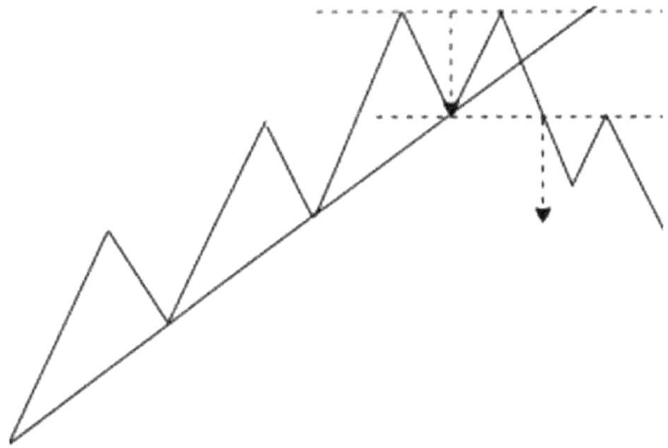

Head-and-shoulders patterns do not happen often as a complete reversal. The second shoulder must clearly fail to reach new heights and move lower than the previous low to confirm a reversal (Figure 6.4). These patterns are apparent throughout a bull market, but when they aren't confirmed they can be a real headache for early short-sellers. When holding a long-term position, head and shoulder patterns should alert you to probable reversal. My frustration with this pattern almost pushes me to eliminate it from the toolbox, but enough traders still use it that it sometimes appears as a self-fulfilling. Nevertheless, still a powerful indicator where longer term trend lines are broken.

Figure 6.4 (Head and shoulders)

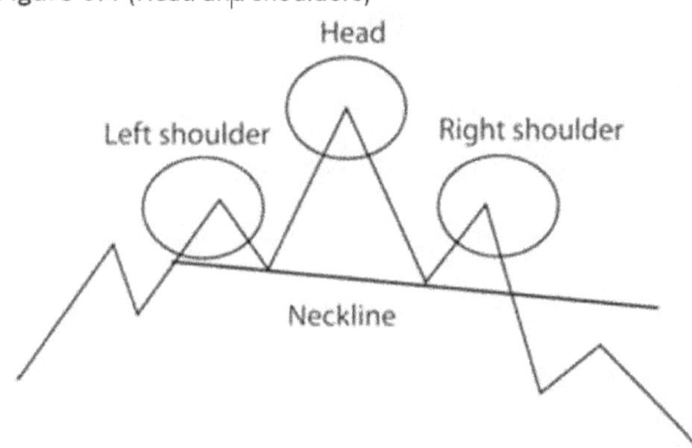

Base-Building patterns are calming for the market, meaning price moves horizontally for several weeks or months. Price equilibrium reduces volatility, producing continual consolidation and returning confidence to the market. Smart money or Institutional traders, build positions along basing-consolidation patterns, as they can load up large positions without moving the market. Institutional players want to reduce their impact on the market when acquiring or liquidating positions. They don't want to tip their hands and allow traders to front-run. Institutional transactions require a laddered strategy (bought and sold in small packages). Retail traders are far more nimble and can unload positions faster. Additionally, individual traders don't have to contend with compliance and management rulings when executing a market idea.

Figure 6.5

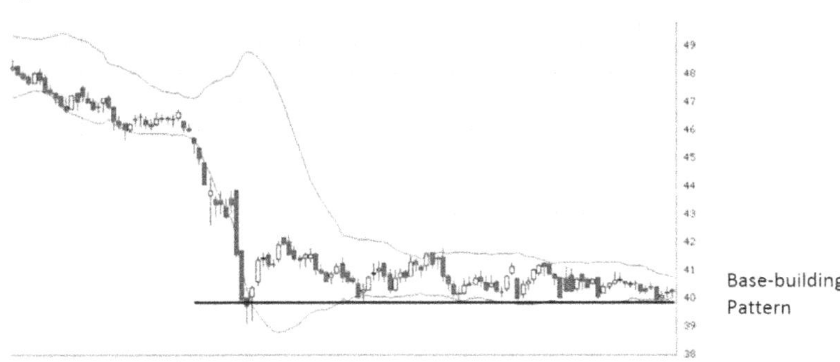

When people say "the trend is your friend", what exactly do they mean? Some proven facts about the market can be observed. Once a strong trend has been established, they persist for extended periods of time. Positive news is incorporated into the trend, while negative news is deflected. Trends usually endure until a greater event or absolute exhaustion is met. This happens when all the buyers have bought or all the sellers have sold, reaching a climax (bullish or bearish). Figure 6.5 below illustrates a textbook bullish movement that lasts for several months to years. In a perfect world every company would have this blockbuster shape. Practice being able to identify these movements. The NASDAQ and other major indexes have rallied in a bullish formation going on 10 years (2018). Pundits argue it's the most hated bull market in history, as would be investors are left behind, and the market keeps going higher and higher. Investor frustration increases for not joining the bull, and as investors capitulate (or give-in), they buy-in at higher and higher prices, sending the market up further. Nevertheless, every bull market has a conclusion and the trend is your friend, but only until the bend at the end. We saw this in 2001, when the NASDAQ blew up and didn't rebound until mid-2015.

Figure 6.6: **Observed Market Truths**

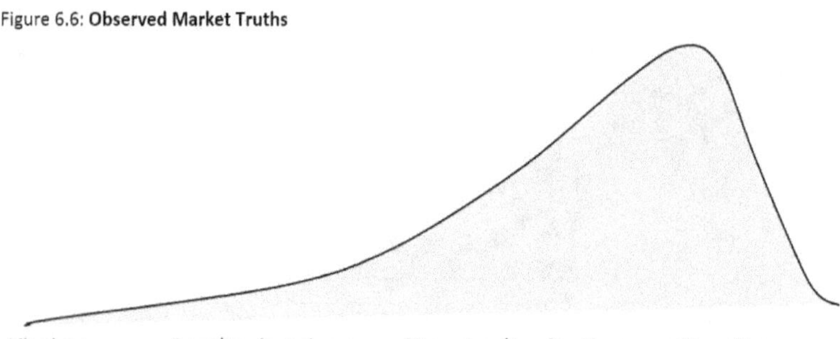

A **Dead Cat bounce** sets-up during a sharp decline. As a stock plummets, investors start buying pushing the price back up. In a Dead Cat bounce, this buying is pre-mature because of a strong downward trend, 9/10 times the price will continue to fade afterward. Holders with a loss above the present market value will create bearish tendencies. Every time the price pushes back up, investors are ready to unload their losses, which restarts the chain of selling. Figure 6.6 portrays a perfect Dead Cat bounce, a short-sellers' delight. The arrow below indicates the bounce and fade afterward. The bounce is considered a trap, and buyers should avoid entering a position at these levels.

Figure 6.7: Dead Cat Bounce

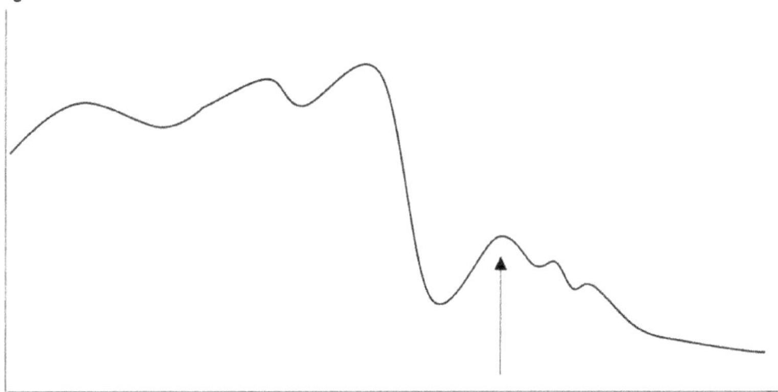

The nucleus of chapters five and six was to break down the complexity of price movement and understanding the buying/selling pressures built into a market. Deconstructing and forecasting price movement is your greatest asset above anything else. Again, the question is - "where was it and where will it go?". Some say historical prices have no effect on future prices. However, tell that to present holders of winning or losing positions. Their **entry point** has an effect on their **exit point**, proving that past pricing is significant. The shapes and levels of a stock/market **tell us a story**. Knowing every part of the story is impossible. That's why we determine price patterns, velocity and the power behind a movement. We need enough information to join early and exit faster.

CHAPTER 7: PICKING YOUR POISON

Investing is all about holding a position for longer periods of time (years). **Trading** has a shorter time horizon. Generally, trades are held for a 1-3 month time horizon and no longer than 6 months. Traders are looking for plenty of ideas, and need to be GENERATING them on a consistent basis (even third party ideas). Don't rely on your favorite investment guru, but listen to their ideas and verify. Don't blindly trade another person's advice or idea. To become an accomplished trader, you need to develop original and unique ideas. We've briefly gone over fundamental/technical analysis, in addition to asset categories. Crossing into successful trades involves great observational skills, and the ability to forecast trends. Essentially, the game is to figure out what's most likely to happen in the future. In reality, we can only **predict** outcomes and nothing is a sure thing. Plan according to what the market gives you, both winners and losers - the only sure-fire technique for trading success.

Traders don't trade in a vacuum – they are part of a global financial system that needs to be appreciated. Your first step is grasping the **world economy**. Read through the headlines on Bloomberg, Reuters and the Financial Times or the Wall Street Journal. Newspapers, magazines, and anything to get you up to speed on what's going on worldwide. Who's bombing who, what are the threats, what are the opportunities? Your trading infancy is all about asking questions. Some obvious things to follow are: **the US dollar, oil prices, interest rates, world stock market indexes, and prices of the main commodity metals: copper, silver, and gold**. Research the historical data of each, which provides necessary perspective. Gold could be trading near all-time highs or 10 year lows. Recounting every number isn't very useful, but the **overall outlook** is what's important. Once you've developed some idea of what the world is, you'll be able to start choosing sectors you're interested in. Maybe you're interested in aviation companies, or maybe it's marijuana stocks. This top down approach of the world is called a **macro view**, whereby a broad perspective is taken in order to narrow-down ideas and opportunities. You'll survive without using this approach, but the big picture matters. I pointed out before that money is in continual motion, moving from one sector to another. A macro view is an interconnected methodology, which connects the dots. The following paragraph illustrates what I'm babbling on about:

A trader's daily summary of thoughts:

July 19th, 2017

> *"The US dollar continues its*
> *downward trend hitting 94 on the*
> *dollar index. Oil rose past $47.00 a*
> *barrel for the first time in a month,*
> *even with oil reserves still high.*
> *Gold is holding steady at $1230/Oz,*
> *while silver gains to $16.50. Both*
> *the American and Canadian central*
> *banks continue to raise overnight*
> *interest rates. The S&P 500 reached*
> *new all-time highs reaching 2470,*
> *bringing the bull market into its 9th*

*year. Technology stocks especially
the FANGs are pushing markets to
higher highs, investors scramble for
growth. Netflix jumped 10% during
market hours after reporting new
subscriptions. Banks are………"*

At first, researching and retaining market information is challenging, but over time it becomes second nature. The paragraph isn't a macro view itself, but a **micro** view that becomes a piece of the **macro** view. Daily market data becomes part of the global macro story. Similar to how daily weather adds up over time becoming a climate. You'll begin to have ideas about longer-term market direction, especially by using charts. Interest rates either promote or inhibit growth, and also indicate the stage in the business cycle. Looking at different market levels (i.e. interest rates and stocks) will allow you to compare markets and get a better overall picture. Identifying correlations and inverse relationships takes longer for a beginning trader simply because they haven't observed enough data points. You're a detective looking for clues along the way, but you need to keep alert in order not to miss one.

Screeners are a quick way to systematically create a list according to a set of parameters you've chosen. Screeners are usually built around fundamental data and can include: the market, sector, P/E, market capitalization, stock price, dividend yield, payout ratios, debt, etc. Figure 7.1 from TMX money website (investing.com has a more sophisticated screener), is an example of a screener I use to scan American and Canadian markets. Once the list is populated, you can choose exactly what you want, with ideal P/E ratio, book value, or other variables. Screeners are an essential tool in any trader's toolbox! Similar to a screener, most brokerages will provide a daily or weekly **bond bulletin**, to help investors locate bond offers, especially fire sale deals on high yield/junk bonds.

Figure 7.1

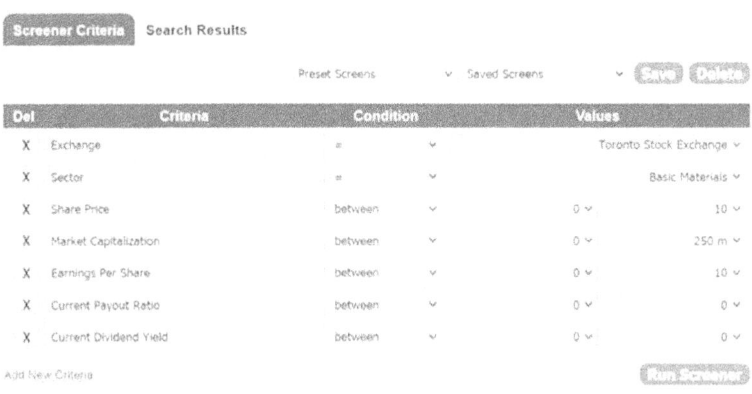

Market movers are lists generated by all major stock exchanges that let you know where the action is. Major selling or buying is reflected by a percentage move, volume activity, or total dollar value. Penny stocks dominate percentage moves, due to smaller values. Be specific when selecting market movers by price percentage, and avoid micro stocks and pink sheets. As these are measures of relative price movement, a crummy little penny stock might go up 120% in one day. Absolute dollar movers are also deceiving as large cap stocks dominate these lists. However, reversals or major continuations are best reflected by volume screeners because of the explosive nature of volume around inflection points. To complement these lists, scan the morning news and company earnings to investigate the causes of the movement further. More often than not, you won't be able to ascertain the precise reasons for a movement. Use your charting and fundamental analysis skills, and remember that price action tells you exponentially more than the news ever will. Every single morning at 9:45 am I check the most active by volume market mover list. This provides me with a picture of the day ahead and tells me which sectors are moving up and which are presenting reversal opportunities.

Financial news, is it any good? There is the saying "you don't know what you don't know". If something is locked up in a box, then nobody can tell you what's inside. The market is a box made up of the opinions (and money) of participants. The financial media wants to sell information to these participants, but how much news is there to sell on most days? Imagine if your favorite financial news anchor began their broadcast with "today the market went up (or down)

1%, which is totally within the realm of probable outcomes". Not very interesting, is it? It's far more entertaining to say "today the market went up 1% because of something some politician said about a trade deal, and this settled the market's uncertainty, because the market hates uncertainty". People hate uncertainty, but that's the only certainty in life! To ascribe a usually made-up reason to the random daily noise of market movements is certainly proof of the existence of 'fake news' in some instances.

You'll need to find media sources you trust – because they stick to the facts without embellishing with their interpretations of those facts. Opinions are like weeds, so pull them out and leave them by the curb. It's obvious that there are thousands of 'experts' persuasively trying to sell their ideas to the market, with forecasts, data and even charm. Financial media relies on these 'expert' commentators who have their own agendas. Overtime, you'll realize who the true stars are, and where the snakes lay. The proverbial 'pump and dump' schemes are best viewed through media dissemination. Stock fads spread out reaching the population with more and more people buying in, until the trade becomes exhausted. This doesn't always result in failure, but major corrections are inevitable if **earnings and financial data don't measure up to the hype.**

Generally speaking, earnings dictate the overall success of a company, which the stock price reflects. Earnings can be grown organically, or through acquiring other companies (artificial growth). Either jump in very early or avoid these plays. Valiant Pharmaceuticals had meteoric appreciation, becoming the largest Canadian company by market capitalization. They did this by purchasing drug patents and companies, rebranding them and tripling the price. What could go wrong? Valeant plummeted from a $300 share price down to $15, and investors were decimated. Traders made and lost fortunes during its rise and fall. Remember money is made in both directions. Recognize these darling names in the media, and be aware of bullish and bearish chart formations. Again, remember the importance of the media in selling stories to investors. If a company is popular with the crowd, what incentive does the financial press have to cast it in a negative light? How would they ever get CEOs on their television programs or quoted in their newspapers if they didn't tend to cast these folks in a positive light?

Skepticism aside, market **sentiment** and overall market bias are highly influenced by trusted media members. For the most part, reporting of financial events is a straight-forward honest pursuit. Sentiment is all about what the crowd thinks - analysts, gurus, advisors, and the dialogue comes together forming a perception, which becomes reality. **Themes** take shape, such as the bullishness toward marijuana stocks or the bearishness toward oil companies. Once these **themes turn into trends**, purchasing accelerates, creating momentum trades. From my experience, early stage momentum plays are the safest bets with the highest returns. These prospects are found by observing the technical channeling formations and excessively positive sentiment. Without a doubt, themes or trends have some financial backing, but market sentiment powered by the crowd pushes valuations to excessive levels. This is why fundamental analysis is so important - being able to recognize bubbles and act accordingly by being a **contrarian** trader/investor. Contrarians arrive first to the party. They identify where the money will flow to next by hypothesizing future trends. Being against the crowd is a lonely and patient journey where trades either coalesce or burn you out.

Once you've isolated some companies that look promising, digging deeper is the next step. Reuters, Bloomberg, Yahoo, and other websites provide **financial statements and statistics**. Accounting information is efficiently presented, perfect for traders who want metrics and data as quickly as possible. For those who want to see the data straight from the horse's mouth, EDGAR in the US and SEDAR in Canada are the online databases set-up by securities regulators to disclose corporate financial statements. Doing an Internet search for 'EDGAR' or 'SEDAR' followed by the company name is a quick way to find financial documents (i.e. 'EDGAR Apple').

If a company looks like it has potential, then your job is to compare and analyze similar companies. Which is the better pick? Who has less debt, a higher cash flow, reasonable dividend yield (payout ratio), high return on equity, net profit, earnings etc. For example, TMXmoney.com or CNBC offer useful bar graphs that display past earnings and future projections. Consistent earnings over multiple years and hitting annual earnings targets show a company with efficient management. A ship doesn't make it past the harbor with a drunken captain. Steve Jobs was no drunk, and he took Apple way beyond anyone's imagination. People generally feel confident with exceptional leaders, which brings calming price appreciation. When a revolutionary CEO departs, the stock price reflects the loss of a valued and remarkable individual.

Developing and Building your Watchlist

Generating and verifying ideas is half the work. Building your watchlist is the next step. I use multiple watchlists depending on the themes I'm following, including a short position list. Beginners should start with one watchlist, so bundle all of your most promising stocks onto the same list. **The companies or ETFs on your watchlist are a reflection of an idea you have, so your watchlist is essentially an "idea bank".** Every trader needs to track and observe price movement, and equity behavior. How does the stock or ETF react in different circumstances? How can you take advantage next time? The core questions on your mind should be timing, as you always need to ask yourself if something is a buy or a sell. After stalking an equity for several weeks to months, you'll begin to anticipate where the price is going. Wannabe surfers go through the same growing pains, with the first waves putting them on their butt. But give a committed beginner some time and he'll be riding the waves by anticipating and feeling the waters in order to 'catch' the wave. **Watchlists act as a convenient standby tool, best used in conjunction with charts and futures.** Build your watchlist by using Yahoo Finance or Google Finance.

Figure 7.2 (sample watchlist)

Symbol	Last Price	Change	% Chg	Currency	Market Time	Volume	Shares	Avg Vol (3m)
EWZ	40.39	+1.76	+4.56%	USD	4:00 p.m. EDT	50.21M	-	35.36M
EEM	38.74	+0.74	+1.95%	USD	4:00 p.m. EDT	99.88M	-	75.93M
G.TO	11.85	+0.03	+0.25%	CAD	4:28 p.m. EDT	7.60M	-	3.08M
DGS.TO	4.02	-0.05	-1.23%	CAD	4:00 p.m. EDT	230.02k	-	203.98k
MU	36.01	+1.35	+3.89%	USD	4:00 p.m. EDT	35.32M	-	36.66M
AMAT	32.42	+1.30	+4.18%	USD	4:00 p.m. EDT	15.14M	-	12.97M
CGC	33.97	+0.90	+2.72%	USD	4:01 p.m. EDT	12.12M	-	13.88M
AMD	17.20	+0.35	+2.08%	USD	4:00 p.m. EDT	99.05M	-	121.95M
CFP.TO	19.24	+0.74	+4.00%	CAD	4:00 p.m. EDT	507.28k	-	465.80k
AC.TO	23.41	-0.44	-1.84%	CAD	4:00 p.m. EDT	1.14M	-	1.26M
FTT.TO	27.63	+0.26	+0.95%	CAD	4:19 p.m. EDT	289.48k	-	441.47k

With your list compiled, the stars need to align, and you need to be watching the skies. Getting the timing right is essential to giving yourself room to succeed. Trades won't always immediately work. Establish a daily monitoring routine where you strategize and anticipate where the market is going. Finviz is a graphical webpage that gives visitors a quick visual overview of world indices, commodities, and currencies. Isolate the variables that have an impact on your watchlist, and identify the opportunities. For example, if oil futures are rising, then the likelihood of energy stocks jumping is higher. Set yourself up with the highest probability for success by picking your entry points. Certain currencies or indexes maybe highly correlated with an idea/stock you're following. So doing your homework beforehand means you'll be well prepared to see a profitable alignment. You always have to be ready to execute your trade because you never know when the market will give you the all-clear signal. Sharp market movements yank along almost every stock, so don't fight against the market - run with it. When a market is persistently falling, **don't grab the falling knife! Wait for the prices to**

settle, then make your move. Enter the market when it's working with your idea, not against it. Half the secret to success in trading (and in life) is getting out of your own way!

Consolidating all your market information with technical charting leads to a well-timed entry. Go over the technical charting chapter again, memorizing the formations and candlestick patterns. Upper indicators concentrate on price, while lower indicators are confirming tools and highlight divergence. People like round numbers (not fractional numbers), so support and resistance levels ('inflection points') revolve around them. Target pivot points, reversals, break outs, and continuation patterns to time your entry. Pulling the trigger takes time and you need **patience** – so don't force it. On the flip side, too often traders suffer from **paralysis by analysis**, and never make a move. Through practice and preparation, your tolerance to uncertainty rises. Even seasoned traders return to the basics to re-evaluate their techniques. Once the entire picture comes together and a decision is made, your next step is **execution**. Entry and Exit is where everything comes to life, where REAL money is on the line.

Note: A regimented plan for choosing equities or bonds sets traders up for success by avoiding emotionally based trades. However, with a practice based intuition we have to be reactive at times to take advantage of opportunities. While analyzing and watchlist-building, diamonds can pass our detection, and the key is reacting decisively once you've found them. Don't let them slip through your fingers.

Another winning approach is basing trades solely on fundamental (value and contrarian) or technical analysis, which isolates your methodology and can lead to better trading. This basically simplifies a trader's approach as too many variables tend to result in humans making unforced errors. Hence my recommendation is for **keeping things**

simple, and recycling the tools you find that work again and again. Success in this industry isn't synonymous with a concrete methodology, so cherry pick what works for you. Even sticking to one equity/stock works for some traders. They learn everything there is to know about the stock, then trade its movements up and down. Even though these strategies simplify trading, two drawbacks are lack of diversity and missing-out on a broader range of prospects. Wearing horse-blinders helps with concentration, but can also increase the likelihood of being hit by a train.

CHAPTER 8: ASSUME THE CONTROLS, EXECUTING YOUR TRADING PLAN

Most trading books lack a chapter that focuses on the actual trade. Novice traders suffer from panic and emotional trading without any forethought. This chapter aims to alleviate or even remove emotion from trading. Being enthusiastic about trading is fine, but when you're executing a trade, you want to be as robotic as possible. When I was teaching, I dreaded showing up in the morning to class with nothing planned. If I did, the students would see right through my incompetent smile and rip me to shreds! In hindsight, I have rambunctious Australian students to thank for making me a very detailed planner. Every single minute was accounted for, and being overly prepared diminished the panic and stress.

You need to set contingencies for whichever way a stock moves. With plan A through Z already formed, you won't panic when things move against you. **Every single trader needs to get comfortable with loss.** When stops (price you choose to exit) hit, you must move forward with the exit. Some traders can use mental stops to exit a trade, but the most robust mechanism is to set a stop-loss when you buy the stock and adjust it as the price rises. For example, if I buy a stock today at $20 and set my stop-loss at $19, then my broker will automatically sell it for me if the stock drops below $19.01. Instead of relying on my own fortitude (which is tough when your money is on the line), I can automate-away the temptation to watch my stock go to $18…$17…$16 all the while saying "when it pops back up, I'll exit… I just need a higher price!" - Rule number one is survival through discipline. Save yourself 20, 30, or even 40,000 dollars, by learning to exit losing positions quickly. When I first started trading, I'd always ask other traders "when do you get out?" Almost none of them had a clear answer for me, and I thought – what idiots! If your trade works out from the start and your stock price rises, then you can always adjust your stop-loss price higher. If it hits $21, then you just move the stop-loss up a dollar from $19 to $20. Using this method allows you to limit your downside while protecting your upside.

Every professional trader works with stop-loss percent or dollar amount-loss limit for every trade. A general rule of thumb is 10%-20% loss for stops, but my mental stops are much tighter at 5% +/- 1%. I cut my losses quickly because I believe that **nothing good ever starts off bad**, which is my mantra for avoiding losses. Your greatest tool for avoiding early stops is timing and giving yourself as much room as you can to work with. Focus on technical analysis for bang-on timing. I choose support and resistance levels because they indicate if you're right or wrong almost immediately. Prices will either move to new heights or fail through support. I'm no gambler, so I **wait** for the market to show me direction. Long red bars and long green bars are my flashing lights to either buy or sell. When high probability formations begin to unfold, they are far less likely to move back against you. A perfect example is during quarterly earnings season. Trader's line up their bets one way or the other, and presto you have winners and losers. Earnings dictate stock movement, and with strong results, a stock will likely continue rising until another variable affects its direction. So I ask "why place your bets before the earnings report?" Bigger gains, yes, but also immediate loss if you're wrong. Taking a winning piece on the way up is a better course of action in my books. **React to sudden changes** - don't place bets beforehand.

So back to our plan, we want to be aware of earnings season before entering any trades. Therefore, you need to forecast how long you'll hold a position. Remember, you're anticipating what will happen one or two steps ahead. Focus on what will help your trade to materialize, not on distant variables. You can hold a flat position for 1 to 3 months before it starts moving up, so give your idea time to play out. Having said that, be aware of idle money that isn't performing. If your plan isn't playing out accordingly and/or hits your stop-loss, EXIT IMMEDIATELY.

Market open and close have the most volume, and action. The 9:30am to 11:00am period is an adjustment and confirming period. Either a stock will continue along its course or it will reverse, usually around 10:30am. The day's **pricing range** is also set during these times, along with the daily direction. Be patient during the first hour, wait and see how the pricing develops. The end of the day brings certitude, especially during the last ten minutes. Institutional players will step in reaffirming trades, or work against them. Use the opening and closing bell to grab some of the better pricing. Ask yourself whether the market is moving with you. Look carefully at figure 8.1, a 5-day chart of Goldcorp. Pay attention to the opening and closing volume, and price action.

Figure 8.1   (5-day Chart, observe lower volume)

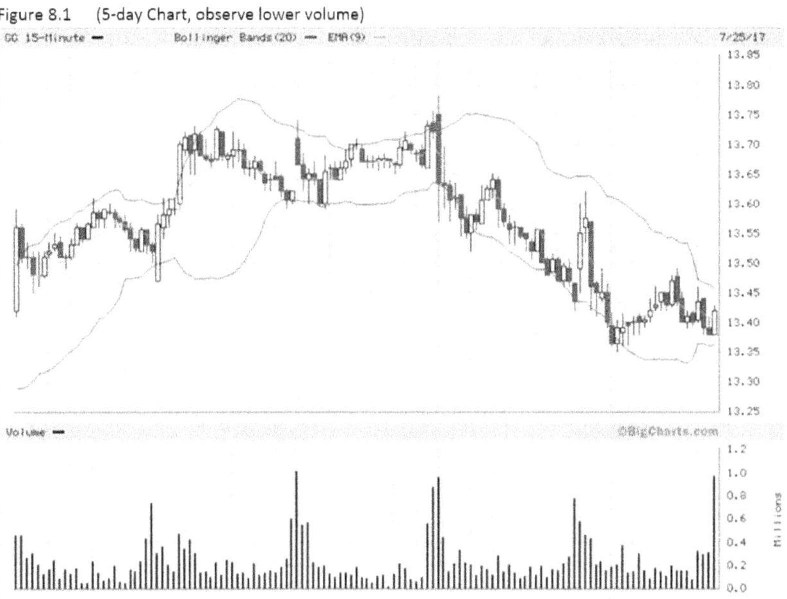

Before entering your order, closely track level 1 quotes to see the real time price. **Level 1 quotes** show the last traded price and the closest matching prices of bid/ask (buyer/seller) on the table. However, plenty of traders place limit orders at completely different prices. **Level 2 quotes** show the line-up of buyers/sellers after the best prices (price, size and number of orders are shown). This gives you a good idea of where the price is going, because remember it's an auctions market. If the buyers outnumber the sellers, prices generally rise and vice versa. Level 2 quotes are especially important for illiquid stocks/bonds. Figure 8.2 shows a sample level 2 quote.

Figure 8.2 (Level 2 Quote)
BOMBARDIER CL B SV (CA: BBD.B)

Real-time

Last: **2.54**   Change: 0.13 ⬆   Volume: **12,644,373**   Last Trade: **12:48**

Level II Quote

	Bid			Ask	
Price	Total Size	# of Orders	Price	Total Size	# of Orders
$2.53	911	26	$2.54	1510	49
$2.52	595	15	$2.55	1383	35
$2.51	1362	19	$2.56	1496	55
$2.50	1464	35	$2.57	3607	57
$2.49	635	9	$2.58	3740	50
$2.48	729	8	$2.59	1257	33
$2.47	247	6	$2.60	8823	177
$2.46	250	9	$2.61	1888	31
$2.45	346	11	$2.62	2063	32
$2.44	125	1	$2.63	60	1

Detailed Trading Plan:

For the nitty-gritty of each trade, you should set up a paper trading slip to help guide you. Below is the trading slip I use (Figure 8.3).

Figure 8.3: Trading Plan: Remember 1/3 risk to reward ratio (e.g. 250/750)

Date:		Time:		Equity:	
Opening Range		Buy limit Sell limit Market	Stop Loss Buy-Stop Stop-Limit	Sell Target Buy Target Trailing Stop	Profit/Loss
Weekly High					
Weekly Low					
P.Day high		# of Shares	# of Shares 2nd lot	Total # of Shares	
P.Day low					
Pivot Point (H+L+C)÷3=		Trade Notes:			
Resistance P1 (2 X P) −L=					
Support P2 (2 X P) −H=					

The right box I've bolded is where you need to start. Don't over complicate the trading slip when you first start. The essential data you need to be concerned with are your buy and sell prices, your stops, and the size of your trade. At the top, write down the time of your trade, which you can use to analyze your trading later. An entry (buy) price is recorded, being a market and limit order. During the open and close, **market orders** (executed at market ask price) are useful for getting in immediately, otherwise you can be left in the market dust. I'd advise you to use limit orders whenever possible, but don't let anyone tell you to avoid market orders all together. Market orders, have a place and time, especially when a stock is on the move or during volatile periods.

Next, enter TWO future sell targets, one being a profitable exit point and the other being a stop loss. The reverse is true if you're short-selling – instead of placing a stop-loss order, you will place a buy-stop cover. If you're correct and the trade is working, you have two choices: either you stick with your hard sell target or you can use a **trailing stop** that shadows the upward progress. Trailing stops trigger when the price drops a certain percentage from the top, and turns into a market order. I have trouble completely relinquishing control to a system, but when you're away from the markets, you need to maintain some sort of control. Discretion and judgement must be applied with every trade, so don't act blindly. The plan is set up to assist you, and bring some accountability to your trading. After veering off the trading path a few times, and feeling a few stings, you'll return to a structured approach. Positions are never supposed to control you – you control your trades!

Traders are risk managers, so the size of your position is the next consideration. Use what are called 'half lots'. If you intended to invest a total value of $5,000, cut it in half and purchase $2,500 worth. If you were planning to buy 200 shares, instead buy only 100 shares. Add another lot if the trade begins to work in your favor. Look for confirmation before committing to your full position size. Once the entire trade is executed, record the profit or loss. Include additional notes especially when you make mistakes. Jotting-down notes is a priority when you're starting out. To improve your behavior, include both positive and negative **reflections**. When I was teaching, I suffered from constant self-doubt and criticism, which improved my performance. I was always striving for the perfect lesson, and now the perfect trade. We're looking for a flawless trade – tenacity serves people well on Wall Street.

Simple enough, right? Wrong! Once the trade is on, the beginning requires constant attention. Like planting a seed that will grow into a towering Oak tree, the first sprouts are always the most important. Losses are to be cut quickly. Winning trades take care of themselves, but trailing stops or hard stops need to be levelled-up as the stock rises. Trade management revolves around **letting gains build and only incurring small losses**. You don't want things getting out of control, remember that an instantly losing trade isn't difficult to get rid of. Just learn the lesson from your mistake and move on. The trickier scenario is when winners turn around on you, reversing from a profit to a loss. To prevent disappointment, use an active strategy called **grooming**. If a position moves against you, at least cover your commissions and even take a small gain. When I say active, I mean you're glued to the screen ready to move.

Intuition and instinct play into the equation, since each situation is different. Linda Bradford Raschke, a genius trader and author, brings together some great tactics. Models she ran prove small gains are statistically more probable than sustained large gains, which is evident to most people. We're always aiming for the homerun, but by grooming and taking small gains, we still win. Think about it, with the proper trading management you only need 5 out of 10 winning ideas to be correct and profitable. To continue the baseball analogy, instead of swinging for the fences on every at-bat, a trader wants to play moneyball and continually drive baserunners home with singles and doubles.

Greed and fear are the underlying emotions constantly aggravating and motivating traders. Begin with small manageable trades that won't leave a scar. With more practice and a proven system, you'll start placing more aggressive trades. **Leverage** (using loans) becomes a consideration in maximizing your entire portfolio. Some traders never feel comfortable borrowing brokerage money (margin accounts). The losses can be substantial and dealing with market calls is a nightmare. Resourceful market participants utilize their margin accounts to increase profits, but only the most skillful can survive catastrophic failures. No ONE trade should ever be able to blow up your account.

Market professionals and business people alike have argued over the path to riches. Conventional wisdom says to diversify, but diversifying reduces losses and profits. Why choose 20 stocks, when you can choose 10 or even 5? Why not just choose the best one? More often than not, conventional thinking keeps people poor – and unconventional thinking makes people rich. When you are impoverished and scratching pennies together, a riskier appetite may be the only way forward. I've always asked myself why would anybody start just one business? The stock market gives you thousands to choose from, and the ability to easily divide resources among them. Personally, 10% of my wealth has never been on a single position, as my appetite just isn't that big. Several years ago a friend asked me about a Litigation Fund paying a 12% dividend. He put his entire fortune on one ship, fully loaded. He'd placed every last penny of his retirement into a single fund and I pleaded with him "reduce your position to no more than 30%" (which was still insane). Several months later I received an email saying he'd lost everything in a Ponzi scheme; Centaur Funds out of Hong Kong had lost hundreds of millions of investor dollars, and all it took to uncover the scam was a simple phone call to the auditors. They said they'd never heard of the Centaur Fund, and had definitely never audited them. The lesson from my friend's mistake is that fear keeps you alive much longer than greed. Always keep in mind the title of former Intel CEO Andy Grove's book: 'Only the Paranoid Survive.'

CHAPTER 9: PORTFOLIO MANAGEMENT AND INDUSTRY DIVERSIFICATION

A sophisticated investor has an assortment of assets that are either producing income or capital appreciation. Winning in trading is all about mitigating risk, and spreading money around to the right places. How often is somebody wrong about an idea? Hence our proactive diversification into many different asset classes beyond the markets. People who are wealthy do not just stick with the public markets, but also buy into physical properties (i.e. real estate or private equity), private placements, gold and other assets. Systemic failures bring down entire markets, and no amount of diversifying will keep you unscathed. System-wide events rarely happen, but sectors and industries are constantly going through **cycles**, from bubbles to vacuums.

Portfolio management isn't just about diversifying, but it's also about reviewing and planning. For traders, time horizons are much smaller than for investors – portfolio monitoring is a weekly event. In addition to generating new ideas, portfolio monitoring involves identifying areas of weakness and strength, so we can add to or reduce positions. Every portfolio should have equities, bonds, and liquid money market instruments (even gold for the paranoid). Elite managers keep a high portion of their capital in equities. As a retail investor, you are nimble being able to buy and sell quickly, which is a life-saving advantage. Bonds and liquid money market instruments are for the rainy days, or when you simply don't know where to put your money. Idle money or 'cash' is still considered a position, but at the very least place surplus cash into money market instruments or high interest savings accounts. Interest and dividend payments add up faster than you think. **The architecture of your portfolio is a personal choice reflecting how you want your financial goals met**. Match your life goals and age to your portfolio. As we get older, conservative choices become common sense. Some centenarians still trade naked options, which come with limitless loss.

Figure 9.1

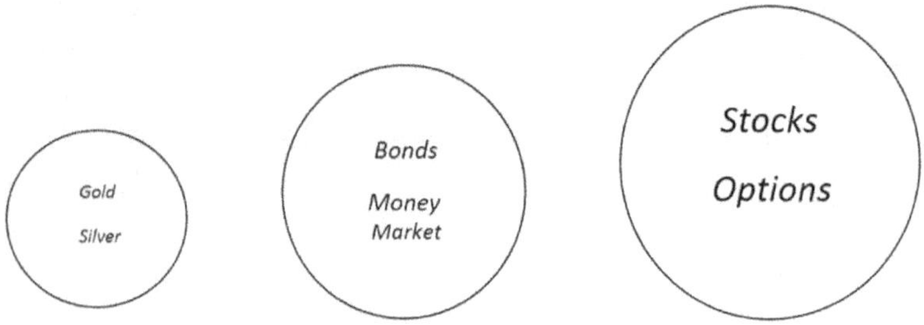

Portfolio mixture: being overweight equities leads to much greater returns

Most people simply can't start off with 10-20 positions, as transaction costs make it out of the question. Considering commissions and price movements, you won't make much on thin spreads. Anything below a $1,000 position should be avoided. Substantial price gains have to take place before any real money is made with such a small position. The cowboys, the risk takers increase the size of a position and reduce the amount of different positions. It's big league bets over diversity, when you believe you're right. Who doesn't want to have the 'confidence' (or foolhardy swagger) to put it all on red or black. Remember, money management and risk appetite work together, and if you lack discipline or clear judgement, a cavalier attitude won't keep you in the game for very long. The flip-side to a single position approach is being over diversified, with too many positions to be able to keep track of. News, charts and other company developments keep you busy, and anything over 30 positions requires a robot. A friend showed me his portfolio with over 80 positions – ridiculous I thought. He's no genius, he'd be better off buying a market linked ETF and go to bed early.

Figure 9.2 (Example Portfolio)

Investments (21 holdings)

↑ Description/symbol	Quantity	Average cost	Current price	Market value	Unrealized gain/loss	Unrealized gain/loss %	Portfolio%
ALARIS ROYALTY CORP - AD	300	18.5832 C	20.57 C	6,171.00 C	+656.05 C	+11.90%	1.79%
BCE COM NEW - BCE	491	42.1925 C	69.08 C	29,009.28 C	+8,291.76 C	+40.02%	9.41%
BMO - BMO	275	57.3798 C	94.61 C	26,017.75 C	+10,238.35 C	+64.88%	7.55%
BMO 3.39% NONCUM FXD FTR PFD S - BMO PR M	200	25.5698 C	24.59 C	4,918.00 C	-155.96 C	-3.07%	1.43%
BMO HISA INVESTORLINE AAT770	66,982.33	1.00 C	1.00 C	66,982.33 C	0.00 C	0.00%	19.42%
BOMBARDIER INC CL B SUB.VTG - BBD.B	6,000	2.4332 C	2.60 C	15,600.00 C	+1,001.10 C	+6.86%	4.52%
BONAVISTA ENERGY CORP - BNP	5,900	5.4896 C	2.93 C	17,287.00 C	-14,623.80 C	-45.81%	5.01%
BROOKFIELD INFRASTRUCTURE PART - BIP.UN	300	19.1332 C	50.91 C	15,273.00 C	+9,553.05 C	+166.08%	4.43%
CHEMTRADE LOGISTICS INC FD TR - CHE.UN	500	15.6178 C	17.44 C	8,720.00 C	+911.10 C	+11.67%	2.53%
ENBRIDGE 5.50% CUM RED SER A P - ENB.PR.A	400	25.7099 C	26.36 C	10,140.00 C	-143.96 C	-1.40%	2.94%
GEORGE WESTON 5.80% CUM PFD SE - WN.PR.A	400	25.4996 C	25.83 C	10,332.00 C	+132.10 C	+1.30%	3.00%
HUSKY ENERGY COM - HSE	255	23.7837 C	14.60 C	3,723.00 C	-2,341.85 C	-38.61%	1.08%
INTER PIPELINE COM - IPL	200	24.35 C	25.04 C	5,008.00 C	+138.00 C	+2.83%	1.45%
MANULIFE 4.65% CL A PFD - MFC PR B	550	22.5834 C	22.65 C	12,457.50 C	+36.60 C	+0.29%	3.61%
MORNEAU SHEPELL - MSI	600	11.8598 C	20.67 C	12,402.00 C	+5,286.10 C	+74.29%	3.60%
PLY TO EXPLORATION & DEV - DEY	300	25.6332 C	20.89 C	6,267.00 C	-1,422.96 C	-18.50%	1.82%
POWER OF CDA 5.6% NON-CUM PFD - POW.PR.A	400	25.3548 C	25.32 C	10,128.00 C	-13.80 C	0.14%	2.94%
SCORPIO GOLD CORP - SGN	1,000	0.89 C	0.06 C	60.00 C	-829.95 C	-93.26%	0.02%
SUNCOR ENERGY INC NEW - SU	340	49.6174 C	41.73 C	14,188.20 C	-2,681.76 C	-15.90%	4.11%
SUNLIFE FIN 4.75% CL A NC SR A - SF.PR.A	800	23.2148 C	22.92 C	18,336.00 C	-235.85 C	-1.27%	5.32%
SURGE ENERGY - SGY	1,950	6.6025 C	2.22 C	4,329.00 C	-8,582.80 C	-55.68%	1.26%

Portfolio exposure is based on market trends, and where capital is flowing. You'd never want to purchase a lagging sector just to have diversity. We're interested in **where the money is and where it's going.** Re-evaluating and monitoring sectors provides a macro view, whereby you can start making predictions and building your portfolio. Below is a daily chart showing how the different sectors performed. Keep track of the numbers below and associated charts. They provide a forecast for future rebounds and continuation. Your portfolio needs exposure to a variety of sectors, and **rebalancing** among these sectors should be changed or adjusted as trends change. The TSX in Canada is highly lopsided, with energy and financial stocks taking up the majority. Don't let your portfolio reflect this. Many oil stock traders learned this the hard way in 2016, when energy stocks lost 80% of their value.

Figure 9.3 (Daily sector performance)

Energy	176.45	-1.27	(-0.71%)
Financials	284.52	0.91	(0.32%)
Health Care	68.84	0.60	(0.88%)
Industrials	216.48	1.94	(0.90%)
Info Tech	62.70	1.75	(2.87%)
Metals & Mining	114.17	-0.64	(-0.56%)
Telecom	167.80	1.66	(1.00%)
Utilities	248.29	0.19	(0.08%)
Aug 1, 2017, 4:42 PM EDT		More Indices ➡	

Apart from sector diversification, strategic themes should also be incorporated into a portfolio. Sectors are horizontal, while **themes are vertical**. Firms within the same sector will typically have more correlation to each other. Sticking to one country with a single market isn't the most intelligent approach either. A calamity within any one country can take out that entire market. When investing overseas, one main consideration in addition to specific country risk is **currency fluctuations**. Having some exposure to another currency through country-specific equities or instruments is both intelligent and prudent. Especially, if local currency is depreciating. For example, Vietnamese ETFs have languished over the years due to the Dong's poor performance. The Nigerian Naira has also been hit extremely hard by falling oil prices, which reduces the performance of any Nigerian company. Strategic choices outside your own country expose your portfolio to unique opportunities and increased variation. From a diversification standpoint, it is usually beneficial to leave your own backyard and look at exposure to foreign markets.

Assimilate a few of these vertical thinking themes into your portfolio:

Figure 9.4 Vertical Themes

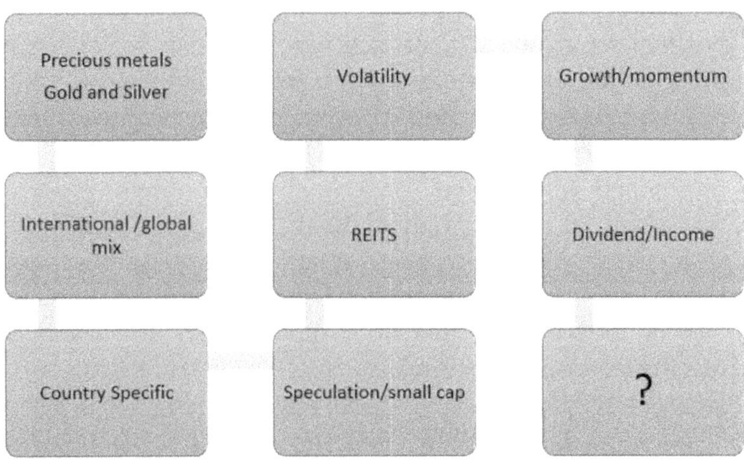

CHAPTER 10: ECONOMIC FACTORS

The stock market's performance is a barometer for economic health. The market meltdown of 2008 foreshadowed the Great Recession that followed. Companies were sold off for pennies, reorganized, went bankrupt, and were bailed out by the government. Business cycles aren't voodoo, they exist! Central banks try to reduce the extreme moves on either end of a boom or bust, by raising and reducing interest rates, and buying and selling assets. Basically, by increasing or reducing the supply of money, Central Banks have a very crude tool with which they can heat or cool the economy. Alan Greenspan tried putting the brakes on the US stock market rally in 2005-2006 by increasing interest rates, but ended up helping crater the economy.

The reason the bubble popped was because the bubble was inflated in the first place. Asset prices had years of appreciation (houses, stocks, land), and investment banks took on way too much risk. Homeowners were over-bidding for houses their wages couldn't keep up with, and stock traders became over-leveraged in their margin positions. When interest rates rose, both groups were left holding very weak hands and folded. When the tide goes out, you see who isn't wearing a swimsuit. The shady characters in the market (think Bernard Madoff) are squeezed in a rising interest rate environment. People hold on to their money instead of investing it, and new capital isn't deposited into funds/schemes as quickly as before. BOOM the scheme falls apart!

As interest rates rise, unsustainable debt simply blows up, and Ponzi schemes are revealed for what they are. The boom-and-bust cycle is normal in a capitalist society, resulting in bigtime winners and losers. However, extreme monetary expansion and record low interest rates have clearly distorted the economy. Raising interest rates in a strong economy allows central banks to mitigate future recessions, allowing them to expand the runway so that interest rates can again be lowered if the economy turns. Central banks around the world have missed the boat on this one, opting to keep interest rates lower for longer. With cheap money flowing like water, expect a longer bull market with a catastrophic ending. Keep in mind, with the accelerated creation of money, its intrinsic value falls. This is a bullish reason to own some gold.

Figure 10.1: The Business Cycle

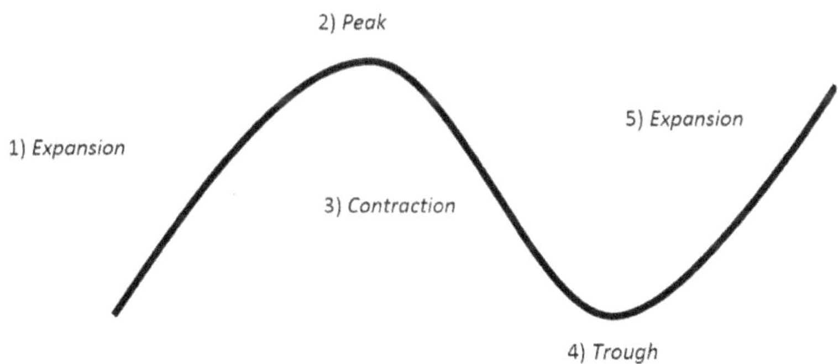

Recognizing the stages of the business cycle, proves helpful when making macro predictions. Different sectors benefit and behave differently at each stage. The stages are: **Expansion-Peak-Contraction-Trough-Expansion**. Stages unfold as society absorbs and dispenses capital. The velocity of money usually indicates an expanding economy and after a bust if the velocity of capital hasn't reclaimed pre-bust levels then money is simply stuck. Predicting future economic health has become virtually impossible, especially with structural and technological changes happening simultaneously with record central bank intervention. No matter what pundits say about the end of risk, asset prices rise and fall, and are forever linked to **interest rates and debt levels**. As a natural contrarian, I want things to fall apart, so I can pick up the pieces. My American friend says to me: "Where there's great chaos, there's great opportunity". Looking into the future, one such decoupling event could take place once central banks unload record levels of assets into the market (namely national bonds). This will result in spiking interest rates as bond prices fall, eventually leading to another recession. Experts talk about an enormous exodus from bonds into equities, but this hasn't yet come to fruition.

Take advantage of these opportunities and avoid the pit-falls by knowing the difference between a secular and a cyclical company. During an expansionary period, miners, industrials, construction, energy and retail tend to do well, as increased human activity is reflected in these **cyclical** companies. New industries find their birth during expansion – identify them and be there early (e.g. marijuana legalization). Cyclical companies suffer during contraction, so you need to sell positions beforehand. Recognize the beginning and ending precursors of each stage. Rotation of smart money moves into secular companies when a recession arrives. **Secular** stocks cover the basic needs of human beings or products people can't live without. People won't go without their ciggies, vodka, or electricity. As a result, these companies fare better throughout a decline. Being in Atlanta in March 2017, I realized I was in the midst of an ongoing expansion.

Evidence was everywhere, housing prices were exploding, imported luxury vehicles were everywhere, and even the most flea-ridden motel room rates were overpriced. Ask yourself when shorting, "what sectors of the economy will be the worst hit in a recession?" Simply look at the wants over the needs. Keep records by building a watchlist that reflects your ideas both short and long.

Economic theories are guiding **principles**, not an exact science. A globalized world has shattered old world economics. The complexity of globalization has reduced the predictability of markets. Aberrations are around every corner, along with geo-political conflicts. China and other emerging nations need to be monitored, and no variable can be overlooked. Major world growth over the last 15 years has not been in the developed world, and this won't change. By most measures, North America and Europe are declining, or at the very least stagnating. Companies who have gained access to the developing world have gained the accompanying growth. Exports and infrastructure spending have fueled the majority of the emerging nations' growth, which will continue. Nevertheless, technological innovation still resides in the West for now.

Consumer Price Index (CPI) is a selection of products and services widely used in society to gauge overall inflation. The fact that it doesn't consider asset prices such as houses and stocks is beyond me. How can the inefficiencies of CPI be relied upon to make policy? Velocity of money is a far better litmus test of an accelerating economy. CPI seems to be a byproduct of a booming economy, a lagging indicator. Traders and investors are interested in **leading** (immediate measurements) not **lagging** indicators (secondary reports). Figure 10.2 begins by showing some leading indicators, followed by coincidental and lagging indicators. Recognizing the cascade of events during the business cycle will help you profit on the downside (short selling). True traders find opportunity from any prevailing condition.

Figure 10.2: Economic Indicators

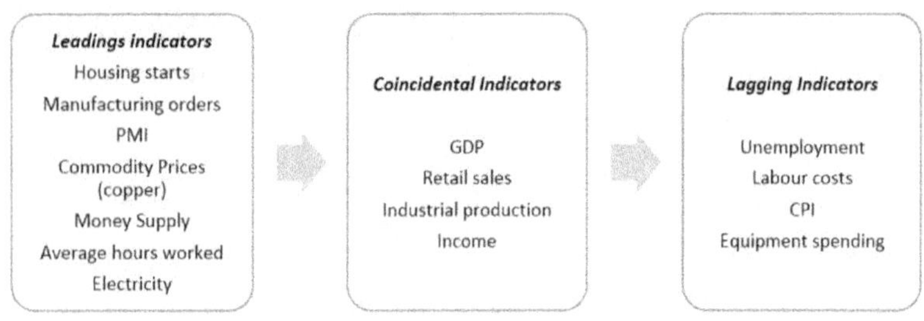

CHAPTER 11: CHOOSING YOUR INTERFACE AND THE TAXMAN

Trading is a game of inches – pile up all those little advantages and your chances of victory are much higher. When it comes to the banks and brokers' bottom line, commissions and trading frequency are paramount. They want you trading and all the time. They're constantly sending educational videos and offering free seminars. They want you feeling comfortable and confident to trade. Platforms are advancing quickly as one stop shops, where all your research is done right on the platform. When selecting your bank or broker, ask for a simulator or a video displaying the platform functions. You want something simple to start, and order entry should be seamless. Placing a trade on some platforms is a chore, with multiple steps where errors can easily occur. Find one that isolates and simplifies order entry, in the form of a pop-up menu or a separate dashboard. Additional features (such as research) come in handy later for generating trading ideas. Generally, you cannot go long and short on the same stock within the same account. So open two accounts or have two platforms with different institutions. Conservative institutions restrict trading activities – shorting specific stocks or exotic assets are examples of where they don't want the risk and won't let you short them. At a minimum, compare a discount broker to a large bank's platform to see what's different. Services and bonus features such as Level 2 quotes can also vary widely.

In countries with banking monopolies, hefty commissions are still part of trading. In the United States, commissions are waived for certain accounts. This is unheard of in Canada where flat rates are the norm. In Singapore or Thailand, commissions are usually percentage based. For those with a million dollar account or making hundreds of trades, special arrangement can be made with a bank to reduce commissions. Discount brokers provide cost efficient structures. For example, Questrade uses a minimum and maximum price depending on volume. Shop around. Reducing your costs is important, especially when implementing the grooming approach. Commissions are a loss right out of the gates, and every inch counts. ETF purchasing tends to be commission-free among discount brokers and some banks, like Scotiabank. Different commissions across different products is another good reason for establishing accounts with two institutions. Interest rates are similar throughout brokers and banks. However, heavily leveraged margin costs eat away at profits over the long term. **A simple and effective strategy is holding high dividend stocks (7% or above), while borrowing at margin rates lower than the dividend**. The investor then pockets the spread between the dividend yield (9%) and interest paid (4.50%). This is a smart strategy in an environment with record low interest rates, but you need to make sure the high dividend is sustainable (i.e. no record of dividend cuts and a payout below 100%).

Taxes trim a significant portion of profits and are the highest cost above even commissions. Take advantage of tax sheltered accounts such as an RRSP or TFSA (401K in the USA). While you should always maximize your sheltered contributions, this is especially prudent if you don't plan on using leverage. Margin accounts aren't tax sheltered for obvious reasons surrounding government tracking and deposit limits. Retirement-type accounts can be burdensome if you already have a generous pension. As time goes by more and more money needs to come out of retirement accounts, which can be heavily taxed. Be sure to extrapolate what you'll need in order to retire. None of us know when we'll kick the can, and an unknown future combined with longer life expectancies leads many retired people to tighten their savings.

Non-registered cash accounts have advantages, such as claiming losses when shares are sold. Also, any interest incurred from borrowing to invest is tax deductible in cash accounts. **Tax sheltered accounts** do not allow you to claim losses, which helps offset capital gains. Once the losses are realized, that's it. You don't get any tax loss credits! If you're implementing a new or risky strategy, a non-registered account might be one way to maximize your upside potential because you can use any losses to offset profit. **Dividend tax credits** are one of the few gifts of tax relief the government gives (only cash accounts, not registered accounts). Without any other additional income, you can receive up to $55,000 in Canadian dividends without paying a single dime in taxes, all outside a tax sheltered registered account. Tax Free savings accounts (TFSA) shelter everything once inside, but income is taxed beforehand. RRSP contributions reduce your present income and, in turn your taxes. On the way out, immediate taxes are collected (withholding taxes). Be sure to withdraw in increments of $5,000 over the year in three month intervals to avoid higher withholding taxes. Annual taxes are still settled up in April, and taxes aren't paid on anything under $11,500 (Ontario residents). Before December 25th, go over all of your positions and decide if tax loss selling is advantageous to you or not. The United States does not observe the TFSA as a tax sheltered account, but does recognize RRSP accounts. Other limited and partnership companies publicly traded incur other hefty American withholding taxes.

Offshoring your money altogether is another gainful way to **legally** avoid hefty taxes. Countries like Luxemburg, Singapore, the territory of Hong Kong and Thailand have ZERO capital gains tax. An obvious move by governments to attract foreign capital and encourage locals to invest. However, being a foreigner increases your credit risk. Therefore, margin and leveraged accounts are more difficult to nail down.

CHAPTER 12: CONCLUSION, THE NON-TANGIBLE

Money is a funny thing. Almost everybody alive has a problem with it, but money doesn't have a problem with anybody. Tolerance to risk will either make or break you, and managing it by having a system you follow is paramount to avoiding emotional swings. Some prodigies have an innate ability after years of practice to guide themselves, shooting from the hip and winning. I'm definitely not one of those people! I live by the structured approach we've gone over, but some circumstances do call for quick action without a definitive planning. Every experienced trader develops a sixth sense or intuition as to where the market is going. I boil it down to your subconscious calculating and concluding the best course of action.

Staying mentally sound and refreshed is imperative to the sustainability of trading. Why bother trading if your life starts falling apart by being up all hours of the night. The purpose of trading is to find some freedom and wealth to lead a better life. Erase the stresses and solitude of trading by getting active. Some push-ups or a walk outdoors will relieve the mind. This sounds like life-coach guru crap, but believe me you'll understand what I mean after staring at a screen for 8 hours straight. The body and mind degrade, and you need to keep your imaginative juices flowing. Set up your own Feng Shui environment, specifically something ergonomic with a comfortable chair and table. Some traders have 9 screens, which is a ridiculous ego boost. I've done well with 2 screens, a tablet and free natural light (avoid dark closets). If you want success then market hours are your life.

A practice account takes you nowhere near the nail biting stresses of REAL trading. Use a practice account for habit building, order entry and motivation. Holding any position exerts a certain amount of stress and anxiety. Always go back to your plan to avoid mentally taxing situations. I previously mentioned setting a time frame. If trades aren't working by the time you expected them to, just drop them. Don't let a position control you. A trade should start taking shape and coalescing rapidly. Sometimes **everything will be working against you**: commissions, a losing trade, and stress. Just when you thought it can't go any lower, it does. Don't ever be surprised by market prices. In the short run, markets aren't anywhere as rational or as efficient as some egghead economists lead people to believe. When things are getting stupid, step back and review the situation as an opportunity. Half lots, grooming and a trading slips are your tools to prevent and mitigate compromising circumstances.

Analysts and the financial media are predominantly biased toward companies, and far more optimistic than pessimistic. Inevitably, every company will eventually go bust. Carefully study and recognize endangered companies. The list of tragic stocks is far longer than need be, from Enron to Valeant to Sino-forest to Nortel. Thankfully, with the advent of the Internet, healthy accusations and condemnations are more common. Market participants are calling companies out, putting them to the fire. Muddy Waters Research, Gotham Research and Citron Research have all helped the public discover Ponzi schemes and fraudulent companies. Short sellers benefit from publicly denouncing companies, so use your judgement and take notice of sound accusations. Clear signs of a sinking ship are **executives departing, accounting/auditing issues (i.e. use of unknown auditors), excessive insider selling, and incoherent executive explanations**. It's easy enough to spot a liar once they're caught red-handed.

Algorithmic and robo-traders, better known as black-box or quantitative trading houses, have significantly increased their presence on Wall Street. Renaissance Technologies is known to use complex mathematical models, which are controlled by computers. There is a revolution unfolding toward active algo-based models. They move faster than any human and can trade thousands of times within minutes. Companies are setting up shop as close to the market center in order to have a millisecond advantage over other "quant funds". These quant funds are generally limited to short-term time horizons, hours to days but more likely seconds. Variables beyond the short-term are too difficult to extrapolate and discretionary human trading still has an advantage in the mid-to-long term range of weeks, months, and years. No matter what an economist tells you, markets are NOT efficient, and holes caused by irrational thoughts plague the system. I'm convinced that with all the instruments, assets, and ideas out there, any trader with enough tenacity can find a winning formula that works for them.

Parting final words: don't gamble your money away. React to movements and be patient. Take what the market gives, because far too many greedy investors/traders have come and gone. Don't follow their path. Bulls make money. Bears make money. Pigs get slaughtered! A win is a win, no matter how small or big. Your goal is to find a proven system that works again and again, with something to show for after you're done. Picking a random homerun like a cannabis stock doesn't make anyone a successful trader. A proven trader pulls the trigger time after time and finds success. Test the market, test ideas, protect your principal, and live to see another day.

- Once you have the key, they've changed the lock -

Managers:

Ray Dalio

Jim Rogers

Linda Bradford Raschke

David Dremen

Kyle Bass

Mohnish Pabrai

Howard Marks

Jeffrey Gundlach

Jim Chanos

Jim Rogers

Linda Bradford Raschke

David Dremen

Jesse Livermore

Steve Eismen

Joel Greenblatt

Larry Berman

Richard Wyckoff

Gary Shilling

Peter Schiff (alternative voice)

Benj Gallander

Websites:

Finviz

Investopedia

SeekingAlpha

Zerohedge

Bloomberg

Stockchase.com

Stockhouse.com

Gurufocus

TMXmoney

Canadian insider

Investing.com

Real Vision

Tradingview.com

Armstrong Economics (alternative voice)

Short Selling firms:

Citron Research

Gotham City Research

Muddy Waters Research

ABOUT THE AUTHOR

Steven Aubin is originally from snowy Ottawa, Canada. He completed his undergraduate studies at Carleton University (Ottawa, Canada) and graduate studies at Southern Cross University (Australia). He has worked for TD Bank as a Trader, and strategized as an Investment Analyst/Trader working for Capital Wealth Architects. The book was inspired by his many years dedicated to trading and pondering the capital markets. He believes that conventional investment books haven't concisely educated traders. His philosophy is to "Get people educated and trading for themselves."

Steven works as a consultant focusing on portfolio architecture, trade themes, and mentoring traders/investors.

Contact Info:

Email: stevenaubin@yahoo.com
Skype: steven.aubin
Twitter: @aubin613
LinkedIn: linkedin.com/in/steven-aubin-22971879
Facebook: Cut the Crap Trader

NOTES

NOTES

NOTES

NOTES

NOTES

NOTES